PENGUIN BOOKS — GREAT IDEAS

Of the Abuse of Words

John Locke
1632–1704

John Locke

Of the Abuse of Words

PENGUIN BOOKS — GREAT IDEAS

PENGUIN BOOKS

Published by the Penguin Group

Penguin Books Ltd, 80 Strand, London WC2R ORL, England

Penguin Group (USA) Inc., 375 Hudson Street, New York, New York 10014, USA

Penguin Group (Canada), 90 Eglinton Avenue East, Suite 700, Toronto, Ontario, Canada M4P 2Y3
(a division of Pearson Penguin Canada Inc.)

Penguin Ireland, 25 St Stephen's Green, Dublin 2, Ireland
(a division of Penguin Books Ltd)

Penguin Group (Australia), 250 Camberwell Road, Camberwell, Victoria 3124, Australia
(a division of Pearson Australia Group Pty Ltd)

Penguin Books India Pvt Ltd, 11 Community Centre, Panchsheel Park, New Delhi – 110 017, India

Penguin Group (NZ), 67 Apollo Drive, Rosedale, North Shore 0632, New Zealand
(a division of Pearson New Zealand Ltd)

Penguin Books (South Africa) (Pty) Ltd, 24 Sturdee Avenue,
Rosebank, Johannesburg 2196, South Africa

Penguin Books Ltd, Registered Offices: 80 Strand, London WC2R ORL, England

www.penguin.com

These extracts taken from *An Essay Concerning Human Understanding* first published 1689
This selection first published in Penguin Books 2009

008

All rights reserved

Set by Rowland Phototypesetting Ltd, Bury St Edmunds, Suffolk
Printed in England by Clays Ltd, St Ives plc

978-0-141-04387-6

www.greenpenguin.co.uk

Of Ideas

Of Ideas in General, and their Original

§1. Every man being conscious to himself, *Idea is the object*
that he thinks, and that which his mind is *of thinking*
applied about, whilst thinking, being the ideas, that are
there, 'tis past doubt, that men have in their minds
several ideas, such as are those expressed by the words,
*whiteness, hardness, sweetness, thinking, motion, man, ele-
phant, army, drunkenness,* and others: it is in the first place
then to be inquired, how he comes by them? I know it
is a received doctrine, that men have native ideas, and
original characters stamped upon their minds, in their
very first being. This opinion I have at large examined
already; and, I suppose, what I have said in the foregoing
book, will be much more easily admitted, when I have
shown, whence the understanding may get all the ideas
it has, and by what ways and degrees they may come
into the mind; for which I shall appeal to everyone's
own observation and experience.

§2. Let us then suppose the mind to *All ideas come from*
be, as we say, white paper, void of all *sensation or reflection*
characters, without any ideas; how comes it to be furnished? Whence comes it by that vast store, which the
busy and boundless fancy of man has painted on it, with
an almost endless variety? Whence has it all the materials

of reason and knowledge? To this I answer, in one word, from *experience*: in that, all our knowledge is founded; and from that it ultimately derives itself. Our observation employed either about *external sensible objects; or about the internal operations of our minds, perceived and reflected on by ourselves, is that, which supplies our understandings with all the materials of thinking*. These two are the fountains of knowledge, from whence all the ideas we have, or can naturally have, do spring.

The objects of sensation one source of ideas §3. First, *our senses*, conversant about particular sensible objects, do *convey into the mind*, several distinct *perceptions* of things, according to those various ways, wherein those objects do affect them: and thus we come by those ideas, we have of *yellow, white, heat, cold, soft, hard, bitter, sweet*, and all those which we call sensible qualities, which when I say the senses convey into the mind, I mean, they from external objects convey into the mind what produces there those *perceptions*. This great source, of most of the ideas we have, depending wholly upon our senses, and derived by them to the understanding, I call *sensation*.

The operations of our minds, the other source of them §4. Secondly, the other fountain, from which experience furnisheth the understanding with ideas, is the *perception of the operations of our own minds* within us, as it is employed about the ideas it has got; which operations, when the soul comes to reflect on, and consider, do furnish the understanding with another set of ideas, which could not be had from things without; and such are, *perception, thinking, doubting, believing, reasoning, knowing, willing*, and all the different actings of our own minds; which we being conscious of, and observing in ourselves, do from these receive into our understandings, as distinct ideas, as we do from bodies affecting our senses. This source of ideas, every man has wholly in himself: and though it be not sense, as having nothing to do with external objects; yet it is very like it, and might properly enough be called internal sense. But as I call the other *sensation*, so I call this *reflection*, the ideas it affords being such only, as the mind gets by reflecting on its own operations within itself. By *reflection* then, in the following part of this discourse, I would be understood to mean, that notice which the mind takes of its own operations, and the manner of them, by reason whereof, there come to be ideas of these operations in the understanding. These two, I say, *viz.* external, material things, as the objects of *sensation*; and the operations of our own minds within, as the objects of *reflection*, are, to me, the only originals, from whence all our ideas take their beginnings. The term *operations* here, I use in a large sense, as comprehending not barely the actions of the mind about its ideas, but some sort of passions arising sometimes from them, such as is the satisfaction or uneasiness arising from any thought.

§5. The understanding seems to me, not to have the least glimmering of any ideas, which it doth not receive from *All our ideas are of the one or the other of these* one of these two. *External objects furnish the mind with the ideas of sensible qualities*, which are all those different perceptions they produce in us: and the *mind furnishes the understanding with ideas of its own operations*.

These, when we have taken a full survey of them,

and their several modes, combinations, and relations, we shall find to contain all our whole stock of ideas; and that we have nothing in our minds, which did not come in, one of these two ways. Let anyone examine his own thoughts, and throughly search into his understanding, and then let him tell me, whether all the original ideas he has there, are any other than of the objects of his *senses*; or of the operations of his mind, considered as objects of his *reflection*: and how great a mass of knowledge soever he imagines to be lodged there, he will, upon taking a strict view, see, that he has *not any idea in his mind, but what one of these two have imprinted*; though, perhaps, with infinite variety compounded and enlarged by the understanding, as we shall see hereafter.

Observable in children §6. He that attentively considers the state of a *child*, at his first coming into the world, will have little reason to think him stored with plenty of ideas, that are to be the matter of his future knowledge. 'Tis by degrees he comes to be furnished with them: and though the ideas of obvious and familiar qualities, imprint themselves, before the memory begins to keep a register of time and order, yet 'tis often so late, before some unusual qualities come in the way, that there are few men that cannot recollect the beginning of their acquaintance with them: and if it were worthwhile, no doubt a child might be so ordered, as to have but a very few, even of the ordinary ideas, till he were grown up to a man. But all that are born into the world being surrounded with bodies, that perpetually and diversely affect them, variety of ideas, whether care be taken about it or no, are imprinted on the minds of children. *Light*, and *colours*, are busy at hand everywhere, when the eye is but open; *sounds*, and some *tangible qualities* fail not to solicit their proper senses, and force an entrance to the mind; but yet, I think, it will be granted easily, that if a child were kept in a place, where he never saw any other but black and white, till he were a man, he would have no more ideas of scarlet or green, than he that from his childhood never tasted an oyster, or a pineapple, has of those particular relishes.

§7. Men then come to be furnished with fewer or more simple ideas from without, according as the *objects*, they converse with, afford greater or less variety; and from the operation of their minds *Men are differently furnished with these, according to the different objects they converse with* within, according as they more or less *reflect* on them. For, though he that contemplates the operations of his mind, cannot but have plain and clear *ideas* of them; yet unless he turn his thoughts that way, and considers them *attentively*, he will no more have clear and distinct ideas of all the *operations of his mind*, and all that may be observed therein, than he will have all the particular ideas of any landscape, or of the parts and motions of a clock, who will not turn his eyes to it, and with attention heed all the parts of it. The picture, or clock may be so placed, that they may come in his way every day; but yet he will have but a confused idea of all the parts they are made up of, till he *applies himself with attention*, to consider them each in particular.

§8. And hence we see the reason, why 'tis pretty late, before most children get ideas of the operations of their own minds; *Ideas of reflection later, because they need attention* and some have not any very clear, or perfect ideas of the greatest part of them all their lives. Because, though they pass there continually; yet like floating visions, they make not deep impressions enough, to leave in the mind clear distinct lasting ideas, till the understanding turns inwards upon itself, *reflects* on its own *operations*, and makes them the object of its own contemplation. Children, when they come first into it, are surrounded with a world of new things, which, by a constant solicitation of their senses, draw the mind constantly to them, forward to take notice of new, and apt to be delighted with the variety of changing objects. Thus the first years are usually employed and diverted in looking abroad. Men's business in them is to acquaint themselves with what is to be found without; and so growing up in a constant attention to outward sensations, seldom make any considerable reflection on what passes within them, till they come to be of riper years; and some scarce ever at all.

The soul begins to §9. To ask, *at what time a man has first*
have ideas, when it *any ideas*, is to ask, when he begins to
begins to perceive perceive; having ideas, and perception, being the same thing. I know it is an opinion, that the soul always thinks, and that it has the actual perception of ideas in itself constantly, as long as it exists; and that actual thinking is as inseparable from the soul, as actual extension is from the body; which if true, to inquire after the beginning of a man's ideas, is the same, as to inquire after the beginning of his soul. For by this account, soul and its ideas, as body and its extension, will begin to exist both at the same time.

§10. But whether the soul be supposed to exist antecedent to, or coeval with, or some time after the first rudiments of organisation, or the beginnings of life in the body, I leave to be disputed by those, who have better thought of that matter. I confess myself, to have one of those dull souls, that doth not perceive itself always to contemplate ideas, nor can conceive it any more necessary for the *soul always to think*, than for the body always to move; the perception of ideas being (as I conceive) to the soul, what motion is to the body, not its essence, but one of its operations: and therefore, though thinking be supposed never so much the proper action of the soul; yet it is not necessary, to suppose, that it should be always thinking, always in action. That, perhaps, is the privilege of the infinite Author and Preserver of things, 'who never slumbers nor sleeps'; but is not competent to any finite being, at least not to the soul of man. We know certainly by experience, that we sometimes think, and thence draw this infallible consequence, that, there is something in us, that has a power to think: but whether that substance perpetually thinks, or no, we can be no further assured, than experience informs us. For to say, that actual thinking is essential to the soul, and inseparable from it, is to beg, what is in question, and not to prove it by reason; which is necessary to be done, if it be not a self-evident proposition. But whether this, 'that the soul always thinks', be a self-evident proposition, that everybody assents to at first hearing, I appeal to mankind. 'Tis doubted whether I thought all last night, or no; the question being about a matter of fact, 'tis begging it, to

The soul thinks not always; for this wants proofs

bring as a proof for it, an hypothesis, which is the very thing in dispute; by which way one may prove anything, and 'tis but supposing that all watches, whilst the balance beats, think, and 'tis sufficiently proved, and past doubt, that my watch thought all last night. But he, that would not deceive himself, ought to build his hypothesis on matter of fact, and make it out by sensible experience, and not presume on matter of fact, because of his hypothesis, that is, because he supposes it to be so; which way of proving, amounts to this, that I must necessarily think all last night, because another supposes I always think, though I myself cannot perceive, that I always do so.

But men in love with their opinions, may not only suppose what is in question, but allege wrong matter of fact. How else could anyone make it an *inference* of mine, *that a thing is not, because we are not sensible of it in our sleep*? I do not say there is no soul in a man, because he is not sensible of it in his sleep: but I do say, he cannot think at any time waking or sleeping, without being sensible of it. Our being sensible of it, is not necessary to anything, but to our thoughts; and to them it is, and to them it will always be necessary, till we can think without being conscious of it.

It is not always conscious of it   §11. I grant that the soul in a waking man, is never without thought because it is the condition of being awake: but whether sleeping without dreaming be not an affection of the whole man, mind as well as body, may be worth a waking man's consideration; it being hard to conceive, that anything should think, and not be conscious of it. If the *soul* doth *think in a sleeping man*, without being conscious of it, I ask, whether, during such thinking, it has any pleasure or pain, or be capable of happiness or misery? I am sure the man is not, no more than the bed or earth he lies on. For to be happy or miserable without being conscious of it, seems to me utterly inconsistent and impossible. Or if it be possible, that the soul can, whilst the body is sleeping, have its thinking, enjoyments, and concerns, its pleasure or pain apart, which the man is not conscious of, nor partakes in: it is certain, that Socrates asleep, and Socrates awake, is not the same person: but his soul when he sleeps, and Socrates the man consisting of body and soul when he is waking, are two persons; since waking Socrates, has no knowledge of, or concernment for that happiness, or misery of his soul, which it enjoys alone by itself whilst he sleeps, without perceiving anything of it; no more than he has for the happiness, or misery of a man in the Indies, whom he knows not. For if we take wholly away all consciousness of our actions and sensations, especially of pleasure and pain, and the concernment that accompanies it, it will be hard to know wherein to place personal identity.

§12. The soul, during sound sleep, thinks, say these men. *Whilst it thinks* and perceives, it is capable certainly of those of delight or trouble, as well as any other perceptions; and *it must necessarily be conscious of its own perceptions*. But it has all this apart: the sleeping man, 'tis plain, is conscious of nothing of all this. Let us suppose then the soul of Castor, whilst he is sleeping, retired from his body, which is no impossible

If a sleeping man thinks without knowing it, the sleeping and waking man are two persons

supposition for the men I have here to do with, who so liberally allow life, without a thinking soul to all other animals. These men cannot then judge it impossible, or a contradiction, that the body should live without the soul; nor that the soul should subsist and think, or have perception, even perception of happiness or misery, without the body. Let us then, as I say, suppose the soul of Castor separated, during his sleep, from his body, to think apart. Let us suppose too, that it chooses for its scene of thinking, the body of another man, *v.g.* Pollux, who is sleeping without a soul: for if Castor's soul can think whilst Castor is asleep, what Castor is never conscious of, 'tis no matter what place it chooses to think in. We have here then, the bodies of two men with only one soul between them, which we will suppose to sleep and wake by turns; and the soul still thinking in the waking man, whereof the sleeping man is never conscious, has never the least perception. I ask then, whether Castor and Pollux, thus, with only one soul between them, which thinks and perceives in one, what the other is never conscious of, nor is concerned for, are not two as distinct persons, as Castor and Hercules; or, as Socrates and Plato were? And whether one of them might not be very happy, and the other very miserable? Just by the same reason, they make the soul and the man two persons, who make the soul think apart, what the man is not conscious of. For, I suppose, nobody will make identity of persons, to consist in the soul's being united to the very same numerical particles of matter: for if that be necessary to identity, 'twill be impossible, in that constant flux of the particles of our bodies, that any man should be the same person, two days, or two moments together.

§13. Thus, methinks, every drowsy nod *Impossible to* shakes their doctrine, who teach, that the *convince those that* soul is always thinking. Those, at least, *sleep without* who do at any time *sleep without dreaming*, *dreaming, that they* can never be convinced, that their thoughts *think* are sometimes for four hours busy without their knowing of it; and if they are taken in the very act, waked in the middle of that sleeping contemplation, can give no manner of account of it.

§14. 'Twill perhaps be said, that the *soul* *That men dream* *thinks*, even *in* the soundest *sleep, but the* *without remembering* *memory retains it not.* That the soul in a *it, in vain urged* sleeping man should be this moment busy a thinking, and the next moment in a waking man, not remember, nor be able to recollect one jot of all those thoughts, is very hard to be conceived, and would need some better proof than bare assertion, to make it be believed. For who can without any more ado, but being barely told so, imagine, that the greatest part of men, do, during all their lives, for several hours every day, think of something, which if they were asked, even in the middle of these thoughts, they could remember nothing at all of? Most men, I think, pass a great part of their sleep without dreaming. I once knew a man, that was bred a scholar, and had no bad memory, who told me, he had never dreamed in his life, till he had that fever, he was then newly recovered of, which was about the five or six and twentieth year of his age. I suppose the world affords more such instances: at least everyone's acquaintance will furnish him with examples enough of such, as pass most of their nights without dreaming.

Upon this hypothesis, the thoughts of a sleeping man ought to be most rational §15. *To think often, and never to retain it so much as one moment, is a very useless sort of thinking*: and the soul in such a state of thinking, does very little if at all, excel that of a looking-glass, which constantly receives variety of images, or ideas, but retains none; they disappear and vanish, and there remain no footsteps of them; the looking-glass is never the better for such ideas, nor the soul for such thoughts. Perhaps it will be said, that in a waking man, the materials of the body are employed, and made use of, in thinking; and that the memory of thoughts, is retained by the impressions that are made on the brain, and the traces there left after such thinking; but that in the *thinking of the soul*, which is not perceived *in a sleeping man*, there the soul thinks apart, and *making no use* of the organs of *the body, leaves no impressions on it, and consequently no memory* of such thoughts. Not to mention again the absurdity of two distinct persons, which follows from this supposition, I answer further, that whatever ideas the mind can receive, and contemplate without the help of the body, it is reasonable to conclude, it can retain without the help of the body too, or else the soul, or any separate spirit will have but little advantage by thinking. If it has no memory of its own thoughts; if it cannot lay up them for its use, and be able to recall them upon occasion; if it cannot reflect upon what is past, and make use of its former experiences, reasonings, and contemplations, to what purpose does it think? They, who make the soul a thinking thing, at this rate, will not make it a much more noble being, than those do, whom they condemn, for allowing it to be nothing but the subtlest parts of matter. Characters drawn on dust, that the first breath of wind effaces; or impressions made on a heap of atoms, or animal spirits, are altogether as useful, and render the subject as noble, as the thoughts of a soul that perish in thinking; that once out of sight, are gone forever, and leave no memory of themselves behind them. Nature never makes excellent things, for mean or no uses: and it is hardly to be conceived, that our infinitely wise Creator, should make so admirable a faculty, as the power of thinking, that faculty which comes nearest the excellency of his own incomprehensible being, to be so idly and uselessly employed, at least a fourth part of its time here, as to think constantly, without remembering any of those thoughts, without doing any good to itself or others, or being any way useful to any other part of the creation. If we will examine it, we shall not find, I suppose, the motion of dull and senseless matter, anywhere in the universe, made so little use of, and so wholly thrown away.

§16. 'Tis true, we have sometimes instances of perception, whilst we are *asleep*, and retain the memory of those *thoughts*: but how *extravagant* and incoherent for the most part they are; how little conformable to the perfection and order of a rational being, those who are acquainted with dreams, need not be told. This I would willingly be satisfied in, whether the soul, when it thinks thus apart,

On this hypothesis the soul must have ideas not derived from sensation or reflection, of which there is no appearance

13

and as it were separate from the body, acts less rationally than when conjointly with it, or no: if its separate thoughts be less rational, then these men must say, that the soul owes the perfection of rational thinking to the body: if it does not, 'tis a wonder that our dreams should be, for the most part, so frivolous and irrational; and that the soul should retain none of its more rational soliloquies and meditations.

If I think when I know it not, nobody else can know it

§17. Those who so confidently tell us, that the soul always actually thinks, I would they would also tell us, what those ideas are, that are in the soul of a child, before, or just at the union with the body, before it hath received any by *sensation*. The *dreams* of sleeping men, *are*, as I take it, all *made up of the waking man's ideas*, though, for the most part, oddly put together. 'Tis strange, if the soul has ideas of its own, that it derived not from *sensation* or *reflection*, (as it must have, if it thought before it received any impressions from the body) that it should never, in its private thinking, (so private, that the man himself perceives it not) retain any of them, the very moment it wakes out of them, and then make the man glad with new discoveries. Who can find it reasonable, that the soul should, in its retirement, during sleep, have so many hours thoughts, and yet never light on any of those ideas it borrowed not from *sensation* or *reflection*; or at least preserve the memory of none, but such, which being occasioned from the body, must needs be less natural to a spirit? 'Tis strange, the soul should never once in a man's whole life, recall over any of its pure, native thoughts, and those ideas it had before it borrowed anything from the body; never bring into the waking man's view, any other ideas, but what have a tange of the cask, and manifestly derive their original from that union. If it always thinks, and so had ideas before it was united, or before it received any from the body, 'tis not to be supposed, but that during sleep, it recollects its native ideas, and during that retirement from communicating with the body, whilst it thinks by itself, the ideas, it is busied about, should be, sometimes at least, those more natural and congenial ones which it had in itself, underived from the body, or its own operations about them: which since the waking man never remembers, we must from this hypothesis conclude, either that the soul remembers something that the man does not; or else that memory belongs only to such ideas, as are derived from the body, or the mind's operations about them.

§18. I would be glad also to learn from these men, who so confidently pronounce, that the human soul, or which is all one, that a man always thinks, how they come to know it; nay, *how they come to know that they themselves think, when they themselves do not perceive it.* This I am afraid, is to be sure, without proofs; and to know, without perceiving: 'tis, I suspect, a confused notion, taken up to serve an hypothesis; and none of those clear truths, that either their own evidence forces us to admit, or common experience makes it impudence to deny. For the most that can be said of it, is, that 'tis possible the soul may always think, but not always retain it in memory: and, I say, it is as possible,

How knows anyone that the soul always thinks? For if it be not a self-evident proposition, it needs proof

that the soul may not always think; and much more probable, that it should sometimes not think, than that it should often think, and that a long while together, and not be conscious to itself the next moment after, that it had thought.

That a man should be busy in thinking, and yet not retain it the next moment, very improbable

§19. To suppose the soul to think, and the man not to perceive it, is, as has been said, to make two persons in one man: and if one considers well these men's way of speaking, one should be led into a suspicion, that they do so. For they who tell us, that the soul always thinks, do never, that I remember, say, that a man always thinks. Can the soul think, and not the man? Or a man think, and not be conscious of it? This perhaps, would be suspected of *jargon* in others. If they say, the man thinks always, but is not always conscious of it; they may as well say, his body is extended, without having parts. For 'tis altogether as intelligible to say, that a body is extended without parts, as that anything *thinks without being conscious of it*, or perceiving, that it does so. They who talk thus, may, with as much reason, if it be necessary to their hypothesis, say, that a man is always hungry, but that he does not always feel it: whereas hunger consists in that very sensation, as thinking consists in being conscious that one thinks. If they say, that a man is always conscious to himself of thinking; I ask, how they know it? Consciousness is the perception of what passes in a man's own mind. Can another man perceive, that I am conscious of anything, when I perceive it not myself? No man's knowledge here, can go beyond his experience. Wake a man out of a sound sleep, and ask him, what he was that moment thinking on? If he himself be conscious of nothing he then thought on, he must be a notable diviner of thoughts, that can assure him, that he was thinking: may he not with more reason assure him, he was not asleep? This is something beyond philosophy; and it cannot be less than revelation, that discovers to another, thoughts in my mind, when I can find none there myself: and they must needs have a penetrating sight, who can certainly see, that I think, when I cannot perceive it myself, and when I declare, that I do not; and yet can see, that dogs or elephants do not think, when they give all the demonstration of it imaginable, except only telling us, that they do so. This some may suspect to be a step beyond the Rosecrucians; it seeming easier to make oneself invisible to others, than to make another's thoughts visible to me, which are not visible to himself. But 'tis but defining the soul to be a substance, that always thinks, and the business is done. If such definition be of any authority, I know not what it can serve for, but to make many men suspect, that they have no souls at all, since they find a good part of their lives pass away without thinking. For no definitions, that I know, no suppositions of any sect, are of force enough to destroy constant experience; and perhaps, 'tis the affectation of knowing beyond what we perceive, that makes so much useless dispute, and noise, in the world.

§20. I see no reason therefore to believe, that the *soul thinks before the senses have furnished it with ideas* to think on; and as those are increased, and retained; so it comes, by exercise, to improve its faculty of thinking,

No ideas but from sensation or reflection, evident, if we observe children

in the several parts of it, as well as afterwards, by compounding those ideas, and reflecting on its own operations, it increases its stock as well as facility, in remembering, imagining, reasoning, and other modes of thinking.

§21. He that will suffer himself, to be informed by observation and experience, and not make his own hypothesis the rule of nature, will find few signs of a soul accustomed to much thinking in a new-born child, and much fewer of any reasoning at all. And yet it is hard to imagine, that the rational soul should think so much, and not reason at all. And he that will consider, that infants, newly come into the world, spend the greatest part of their time in sleep, and are seldom awake, but when either hunger calls for the teat, or some pain, (the most importunate of all sensations) or some other violent impression on the body, forces the mind to perceive, and attend to it. He, I say, who considers this, will, perhaps, find reason to imagine, that a *fœtus in the mother's womb, differs not much from the state of a vegetable*; but passes the greatest part of its time without perception or thought, doing very little, but sleep in a place, where it needs not seek for food, and is surrounded with liquor, always equally soft, and near of the same temper; where the eyes have no light, and the ears, so shut up, are not very susceptible of sounds; and where there is little or no variety, or change of objects, to move the senses.

§22. Follow a *child* from its birth, and observe the alterations that time makes, and you shall find, as the mind by the senses comes more and more to be furnished with ideas, it comes to be more and more awake; thinks more, the more it has matter to think on. After some time, it begins to know the objects, which being most familiar with it, have made lasting impressions. Thus it comes, by degrees, to know the persons it daily converses with, and distinguish them from strangers; which are instances and effects of its coming to retain and distinguish the ideas the senses convey to it: and so we may observe, how the mind, *by degrees*, improves in these, and *advances* to the exercise of those other faculties of *enlarging*, *compounding*, and *abstracting* its ideas, and of reasoning about them, and reflecting upon all these, of which, I shall have occasion to speak more hereafter.

§23. If it shall be demanded then, *when a man begins to have any ideas?* I think, the true answer is, when he first has any *sensation*. For since there appear not to be any ideas in the mind, before the senses have conveyed any in, I conceive that ideas in the understanding, are coeval with *sensation*; which is such an impression or motion, made in some part of the body, as produces some perception in the understanding. 'Tis about these impressions made on our senses by outward objects, that the mind seems first to employ itself in such operations as we call *perception*, *remembering*, *consideration*, *reasoning*, etc.

§24. In time, the mind comes to reflect *The original of all* on its own *operations*, about the ideas got *our knowledge* by *sensation*, and thereby stores itself with a new set of ideas, which I call ideas of *reflection*. These are the *impressions* that are made on our *senses* by outward objects, that are extrinsical to the mind; and *its own operations*, proceeding from powers intrinsical and proper to itself, which when reflected on by itself, become also objects of its contemplation, are, as I have said, *the original of all knowledge*. Thus the first capacity of human intellect, is, That the mind is fitted to receive the impressions made on it; either, through the *senses*, by outward objects; or by its own operations, when it *reflects* on them. This is the first step a man makes towards the discovery of anything, and the groundwork, whereon to build all those notions, which ever he shall have naturally in this world. All those sublime thoughts, which tower above the clouds, and reach as high as heaven itself, take their rise and footing here: in all that great extent wherein the mind wanders, in those remote speculations, it may seem to be elevated with, it stirs not one jot beyond those ideas, which *sense* or *reflection*, have offered for its contemplation.

In the reception of simple ideas, the understanding is for the most part passive §25. In this part, the *understanding* is merely *passive*; and whether or no, it will have these beginnings, and as it were materials of knowledge, is not in its own power. For the objects of our senses, do, many of them, obtrude their particular ideas upon our minds, whether we will or no: and the operations of our minds, will not let us be without, at least some obscure notions of them. No man can be wholly ignorant of what he does, when he thinks. These *simple* ideas, when offered to the mind, *the understanding can* no more refuse to have, nor alter, when they are imprinted, nor blot them out, and make new ones itself, than a mirror can refuse, alter, or obliterate the images or ideas, which, the objects set before it, do therein produce. As the bodies that surround us, do diversely affect our organs, the mind is forced to receive the impressions; and cannot avoid the perception of those ideas that are annexed to them.

[. . .]

Of Simple Ideas

§1. The better to understand the nature, manner, and extent of our knowledge, one thing is carefully to be observed, concerning the ideas we have; and that is, that *some* of them are *simple*, and *some complex*.

Uncompounded appearances

Though the qualities that affect our senses, are, in the things themselves, so united and blended, that there is no separation, no distance between them; yet 'tis plain, the ideas they produce in the mind, enter by the senses simple and unmixed. For though the sight and touch often take in from the same object, at the same time, different ideas; as a man sees at once motion and colour; the hand feels softness and warmth in the same piece of wax: yet the simple ideas thus united in the same subject, are as perfectly distinct, as those that come in by different senses. The coldness and hardness, which a man feels in a piece of *ice*, being as distinct ideas in the mind, as the smell and whiteness of a lily; or as the taste of sugar, and smell of a rose: and there is nothing can be plainer to a man, than the clear and distinct perception he has of those simple ideas; which being each in itself uncompounded, contains in it nothing but *one uniform appearance*, or conception in the mind, and is not distinguishable into different ideas.

The mind can neither make nor destroy them §2. These simple ideas, the materials of all our knowledge, are suggested and furnished to the mind, only by those two ways above mentioned, *viz. sensation* and *reflection*. When the understanding is once stored with these simple ideas, it has the power to repeat, compare, and unite them even to an almost infinite variety, and so can make at pleasure new complex ideas. But it is not in the power of the most exalted wit, or enlarged understanding, by any quickness or variety of thought, to *invent or frame one new simple idea* in the mind, not taken in by the ways before mentioned: nor can any force of the understanding, *destroy* those that are there. The dominion of man, in this little world of his own understanding, being muchwhat the same, as it is in the great world of visible things; wherein his power, however managed by art and skill, reaches no further, than to compound and divide the materials, that are made to his hand; but can do nothing towards the making the least particle of new matter, or destroying one atom of what is already in being. The same inability, will everyone find in himself, who shall go about to fashion in his understanding any simple idea, not received in by his senses, from external objects; or by reflection from the operations of his own mind about them. I would have anyone try to fancy any taste, which had never affected his palate; or frame the idea of a scent, he had never smelt: and when he can do this I will also conclude, that a blind man hath ideas of colours, and a deaf man true distinct notions of sounds.

§3. This is the reason why, though we cannot believe it impossible to God, to make a creature with other organs, and more ways to convey into the understanding the notice of corporeal things than those five, as they are usually counted, which he has given to man: yet I think, it is *not possible*, for anyone *to imagine* any other *qualities* in bodies, howsoever constituted, whereby they can be taken notice of, besides sounds, tastes, smells, visible and tangible qualities. And had mankind been made with but four senses, the qualities then, which are the object of the fifth sense, had been as far from our notice, imagination, and conception, as now any *belonging to a sixth, seventh, or eighth sense*, can possibly be: which, whether yet some other creatures, in some other parts of this vast, and stupendous universe, may not have, will be a great presumption to deny. He that will not set himself proudly at the top of all things; but will consider the immensity of this fabric, and the great variety, that is to be found in this little and inconsiderable part of it, which he has to do with, may be apt to think, that in other mansions of it, there may be other, and different intelligent beings, of whose faculties, he has as little knowledge or apprehension, as a worm shut up in one drawer of a cabinet, hath of the senses or understanding of a man; such variety and excellency, being suitable to the wisdom and power of the maker. I have here followed the common opinion of man's having but five senses; though, perhaps, there may be justly counted more; but either supposition serves equally to my present purpose.

[. . .]

Of Complex Ideas

Made by the mind out of simple ones §1. We have hitherto considered those ideas, in the reception whereof, the mind is only passive, which are those simple ones received from *sensation* and *reflection* before-mentioned, whereof the mind cannot make one to itself, nor have any idea which does not wholly consist of them. But as the mind is wholly passive in the reception of all its simple ideas, so it exerts several acts of its own, whereby out of its simple ideas, as the materials and foundations of the rest, the other are framed. The acts of the mind wherein it exerts its power over its simple ideas are chiefly these three, 1. combining several simple ideas into one compound one, and thus all complex ideas are made. 2. The second is bringing two ideas, whether simple or complex, together; and setting them by one another, so as to take a view of them at once, without uniting them into one; by which way it gets all its ideas of relations. 3. The third is separating them from all other ideas that accompany them in their real existence; this is called *abstraction*: And thus all its general ideas are made. This shows man's power, and its way of operation, to be muchwhat the same in the material and intellectual world. For the materials in both being such as he has no power over, either to make or destroy, all that man can do, is either to unite them together, or to set them by one another, or wholly separate them. I shall here begin with the first of these in the consideration of complex ideas, and come to the other two in their due places. As simple ideas are observed to exist in several combinations united together; so the mind has a power to consider several of them united together, as one idea; and that not only as they are united in external objects, but as itself has joined them. Ideas thus made up of several simple ones put together, I call *complex*; such as are *beauty, gratitude, a man, an army, the universe*; which though complicated of various simple ideas, or *complex* ideas made up of simple ones, yet are, when the mind pleases, considered each by itself, as one entire thing, and signified by one name.

§2. In this faculty of repeating and joining *Made voluntarily* together its ideas, the mind has great power in varying and multiplying the objects of its thoughts, infinitely beyond what *sensation* or *reflection* furnished it with: but all this still confined to those simple ideas, which it received from those two sources, and which are the ultimate materials of all its compositions. For simple ideas are all from things themselves; and of these *the mind can* have no more, nor other than what are suggested to it. It can have no other ideas of sensible qualities than what come from without by the senses; nor any ideas of other kind of operations of a thinking substance, than what it finds in itself: but when it has once got these simple ideas, it is not confined barely to observation, and what offers itself from without; it can, by its own power, put together those ideas it has, and *make new complex ones*, which it never received so united.

§3. *Complex* ideas, however compounded *Are either modes,* and decompounded, though their number *substances, or* be infinite, and the variety endless, where- *relations* with they fill, and entertain the thoughts of men;

yet, I think, they may be all reduced under these three heads.

1. *Modes.*
2. *Substances.*
3. *Relations.*

Modes   §4. First, *modes* I call such complex ideas, which however compounded, contain not in them the supposition of subsisting by themselves, but are considered as dependences on, or affections of substances; such are the ideas signified by the words *triangle*, *gratitude*, *murder*, *etc*. And if in this I use the word *mode*, in somewhat a different sense from its ordinary signification, I beg pardon; it being unavoidable in discourses, differing from the ordinary received notions, either to make new words, or to use old words in somewhat a new signification, the latter whereof, in our present case, is perhaps the more tolerable of the two.

Simple and mixed   §5. Of these *modes*, there are two sorts,
modes   which deserve distinct consideration. First, there are some which are only variations, or different combinations of the same simple idea, without the mixture of any other, as a dozen, or score; which are nothing but the ideas of so many distinct units added together, and these I call *simple modes*, as being contained within the bounds of one simple idea. Secondly, there are others compounded of simple ideas of several kinds, put together to make one complex one; *v.g. beauty*, consisting of a certain composition of colour and figure, causing delight in the beholder; *theft*, which being the concealed

change of the possession of anything, without the consent of the proprietor, contains, as is visible, a combination of several ideas of several kinds; and these I call *mixed modes*.

§6. Secondly, the ideas of *substances* are such combinations of simple ideas, as are taken to represent distinct particular things subsisting by themselves; in which the supposed, or confused idea of substance, such as it is, is always the first and chief. Thus, if to substance be joined the simple idea of a certain dull whitish colour, with certain degrees of weight, hardness, ductility, and fusibility, we have the idea of *lead*; and a combination of the ideas of a certain sort of figure, with the powers of motion, thought, and reasoning, joined to substance, make the ordinary idea of *a man*. Now, of substances also, there are two sorts of ideas; one of single substances, as they exist separately, as of *a man*, or *a sheep*; the other of several of those put together as an *army* of men, or *flock* of sheep; which *collective ideas of several substances* thus put together, are as much each of them one single idea, as that of a man, or an unit. *Substances single or collective*

§7. Thirdly, the last sort of complex ideas, is that we call *relation*, which consists in the consideration and comparing one idea with another: of these several kinds, we shall treat in their order. *Relation*

§8. If we will trace the progress of our minds, and with attention observe how it repeats, adds together, and unites its simple ideas received from sensation or reflection, it will lead us further than at first, perhaps, we should have imagined. And, I believe, we shall find, if we warily observe the originals of our *The abstrusest ideas from the two sources* notions, that even *the most abstruse ideas*, how remote soever they may seem from sense, or from any operation of our own minds, are yet only such, as the understanding frames to itself, by repeating and joining together ideas, that it had either from objects of sense, or from its own operations about them: so that those even large *and abstract ideas, are derived from sensation, or reflection*, being no other than what the mind, by the ordinary use of its own faculties, employed about ideas received from objects of sense, or from the operations it observes in itself about them, may, and does attain unto. This I shall endeavour to show in the ideas we have of *space, time*, and *infinity*, and some few other, that seem the most remote from those originals.

Of Modes of Pleasure and Pain

Pleasure and pain §1. Amongst the simple ideas, which we
simple ideas receive both from *sensation* and *reflection*,
pain and *pleasure* are two very considerable ones. For as in the body, there is sensation barely in itself, or accompanied with *pain* or *pleasure*; so the thought, or perception of the mind is simply so, or else accompanied also with *pleasure* or *pain*, delight, or trouble, call it how you please. These, like other simple ideas, cannot be described, nor their names defined; the way of knowing them, is, as of the simple ideas of the senses, only by experience. For to define them by the presence of good or evil, is no otherwise to make them known to us, than by making us reflect on what we feel in ourselves, upon

the several and various operations of good and evil upon our minds, as they are differently applied to, or considered by us.

§2. Things then are good or evil, only   *Good and evil, what* in reference to pleasure or pain. That we call *good*, which *is apt to cause or increase pleasure, or diminish pain in us; or else to procure, or preserve us the possession of any other good, or absence of any evil.* And on the contrary, we name that *evil*, which *is apt to produce or increase any pain, or diminish any pleasure in us; or else to procure us any evil, or deprive us of any good.* By pleasure and pain, I must be understood to mean of body or mind, as they are commonly distinguished; though in truth, they be only different constitutions of the mind, sometimes occasioned by disorder in the body, sometimes by thoughts of the mind.

§3. *Pleasure* and *pain*, and that which   *Our passions moved* causes them, good and evil, are the hinges   *by good and evil* on which our *passions* turn: and if we reflect on ourselves, and observe how these, under various considerations, operate in us; what modifications or tempers of mind, what internal sensations (if I may so call them,) they produce in us, we may thence form to ourselves the ideas of our *passions*.

§4. Thus anyone reflecting upon the thought he   *Love* has of the delight, which any present, or absent thing is apt to produce in him, has the idea we call *love*. For when a man declares in autumn, when he is eating them, or in spring, when there are none, that he *loves* grapes, it is no more, but that the taste of grapes delights him; let an alteration of health or constitution destroy the delight of their taste, and he then can be said to *love* grapes no longer.

Hatred   §5. On the contrary, the thought of the pain, which anything present or absent is apt to produce in us, is what we call *hatred*. Were it my business here, to inquire any further than into the bare ideas of our passions, as they depend on different modifications of pleasure and pain, I should remark, that our *love* and *hatred* of inanimate insensible beings, is commonly founded on that pleasure and pain which we receive from their use and application any way to our senses, though with their destruction: but *hatred* or *love*, to beings capable of happiness or misery, is often the uneasiness or delight, which we find in ourselves arising from a consideration of their very being, or happiness. Thus the being and welfare of a man's children or friends, producing constant delight in him, he is said constantly to *love* them. But it suffices to note, that our ideas of *love* and *hatred*, are but the dispositions of the mind, in respect of pleasure and pain in general, however caused in us.

Desire   §6. The uneasiness a man finds in himself upon the absence of anything, whose present enjoyment carries the idea of delight with it, is that we call *desire*, which is greater or less, as that uneasiness is more or less vehement. Where, by the by, it may perhaps be of some use to remark, that the chief if not only spur to human industry and action, is uneasiness. For whatever good is proposed, if its absence carries no displeasure nor pain with it; if a man be easy and content without it, there is no desire of it, nor endeavour after it; there is no more but a bare *velleity*, the term used to signify the lowest degree of desire, and that which is next to none at all, when there is so little uneasiness in the absence of anything, that it carries a man no further than some faint wishes for it, without any more effectual or vigorous use of the means to attain it. *Desire* also is stopped or abated by the opinion of the impossibility or unattainableness of the good proposed, as far as the uneasiness is cured or allayed by that consideration. This might carry our thoughts further, were it seasonable in this place.

§7. *Joy* is a delight of the mind, from the consider-   *Joy* ation of the present or assured approaching possession of a good; and we are then possessed of any good, when we have it so in our power, that we can use it when we please. Thus a man almost starved, has *joy* at the arrival of relief, even before he has the pleasure of using it: and a father, in whom the very well-being of his children causes delight, is always, as long as his children are in such a state, in the possession of that good; for he needs but to reflect on it to have that pleasure.

§8. *Sorrow* is uneasiness in the mind, upon the   *Sorrow* thought of a good lost, which might have been enjoyed longer; or the sense of a present evil.

§9. *Hope* is that pleasure in the mind, which every-   *Hope* one finds in himself, upon the thought of a profitable future enjoyment of a thing, which is apt to delight him.

§10. *Fear* is an uneasiness of the mind, upon the   *Fear* thought of future evil likely to befall us.

§11. *Despair* is the thought of the unattain-   *Despair* ableness of any good, which works differently in men's minds, sometimes producing uneasiness or pain, sometimes rest and indolency.

Anger §12. *Anger* is uneasiness or discomposure of the mind, upon the receipt of any injury, with a present purpose of revenge.

Envy §13. *Envy* is an uneasiness of mind, caused by the consideration of a good we desire, obtained by one, we think should not have had it before us.

What passions all men have §14. These two last, *envy* and *anger*, not being caused by pain and pleasure simply in themselves, but having in them some mixed considerations of ourselves and others, are not therefore to be found in all men, because those other parts of valuing their merits, or intending revenge, is wanting in them: but all the rest terminated purely in pain and pleasure, are, I think, to be found in all men. For we *love, desire, rejoice,* and *hope,* only in respect of pleasure; we *hate, fear,* and *grieve* only in respect of pain ultimately: in fine, all these passions are moved by things, only as they appear to be the causes of pleasure and pain, or to have pleasure or pain some way or other annexed to them. Thus we extend our hatred usually to the subject, (at least if a sensible or voluntary agent,) which has produced pain in us, because the fear it leaves, is a constant pain: but we do not so constantly love what has done us good; because pleasure operates not so strongly on us, as pain; and because we are not so ready to have hope, it will do so again. But this by the by.

Pleasure and pain what §15. By *pleasure* and *pain,* delight and uneasiness, I must all along be understood (as I have above intimated) to mean, not only bodily pain and pleasure, but whatsoever *delight* or *uneasiness* is felt by us, whether arising from any grateful, or unacceptable sensation or reflection.

§16. 'Tis further to be considered, that in reference to the passions, the removal or *lessening of a pain is* considered, and operates as a *pleasure*: and the loss or diminishing of a pleasure, as a pain.

§17. The passions too have most of them in most persons operations on the body, and cause various changes in it: which not being always sensible, do not make a necessary part of the idea of each passion. For *shame*, which is an uneasiness of the mind, upon the thought of having done something, which is indecent, or will lessen the valued esteem, which others have for us, has not always blushing accompanying it.

Shame

§18. I would not be mistaken here, as if I meant this as a discourse of the *passions*; they are *many more than those* I have here named: and those I have taken notice of, would each of them require a much larger,

These instances to show how our ideas of the passions are got from sensation and reflection

and more accurate discourse. I have only mentioned these here, as so many instances of modes of pleasure and pain resulting in our minds, from various considerations of good and evil. I might, perhaps, have instanced in other modes of pleasure and pain more simple than these, as the pain of *hunger* and *thirst*, and the pleasure of eating and drinking to remove them; the pain of tender eyes, and the pleasure of music; pain from captious uninstructive wrangling, and the pleasure of rational conversation with a friend, or of well directed study in the search and discovery of truth. But the passions being of much more concernment to us, I rather made choice to instance in them, and show how the ideas we have of them, are derived from sensation and reflection.

[. . .]

Of Adequate and Inadequate Ideas

Adequate ideas, are such as perfectly represent their archetypes

§1. Of our real ideas some are adequate, and some are inadequate. Those I call *adequate*, which perfectly represent those archetypes which the mind supposes them taken from; which it intends them to stand for, and to which it refers them. *Inadequate* ideas are such, which are but a partial, or incomplete representation of those archetypes to which they are referred. Upon which account it is plain,

Simple ideas all adequate

§2. *First*, that *all our simple ideas are adequate*. Because being nothing but the effects of certain powers in things, fitted and ordained by GOD, to produce such sensations in us, they cannot but be correspondent and adequate to those powers: and we are sure they agree to the reality of things. For if sugar produce in us the ideas which we call whiteness, and sweetness, we are sure there is a power in sugar to produce those ideas in our minds, or else they could not have been produced by it. And so each sensation answering the power that operates on any of our senses, the idea so produced, is a real idea, (and not a fiction of the mind, which has no power to produce any simple idea;) and cannot but be adequate, since it ought only to answer that power: and so all simple ideas are adequate. 'Tis true, the things producing in us these simple ideas, are but few of them denominated by us, as if they were only the causes of them; but as if those ideas were real beings in them. For though fire be called painful to the touch, whereby is signified the power of producing in us the idea of pain; yet it is denominated also light, and hot; as if light and heat, were really something in the fire, more than a power to excite these ideas in us; and therefore are called *qualities* in, or of the fire. But these being nothing, in truth, but powers to excite such ideas in us, I must, in that sense, be understood, when I speak of secondary *qualities*, as being in things; or of their ideas, as being in the objects that excite them in us. Such ways of speaking, though accommodated to the vulgar notions, without which one cannot be well understood; yet truly signify nothing, but those powers which are in things, to excite certain sensations or ideas in us. Since were there no fit organs to receive the impressions fire makes on the sight and touch; nor a mind joined to those organs to receive the ideas of light and heat, by those impressions from the fire, or the Sun, there would yet be no more light or heat in the world, than there would be pain, if there were no sensible creature to feel it, though the Sun should continue just as it is now, and Mount Ætna flame higher than ever it did. Solidity, and extension, and the termination of it, figure, with motion and rest, whereof we have the ideas, would be really in the world as they are, whether there were any sensible being to perceive them, or no: and therefore those we have reason to look on, as the real modifications of matter; and such as are the exciting causes of all our various sensations from bodies. But this being an inquiry not belonging to this place, I shall enter no further into it, but proceed to show, what complex ideas are *adequate*, and what not.

Modes are all §3. *Secondly,* our *complex ideas of modes,* being
adequate voluntary collections of simple ideas, which the mind puts together, without reference to any real archetypes, or standing patterns, existing anywhere, *are* and cannot but be *adequate* ideas. Because they not being intended for copies of things really existing, but for archetypes made by the mind, to rank and denominate things by, cannot want anything; they having each of them that combination of ideas, and thereby that perfection which the mind intended they should: so that the mind acquiesces in them, and can find nothing wanting. Thus by having the idea of a figure, with three sides meeting at three angles, I have a complete idea, wherein I require nothing else to make it perfect. That the mind is satisfied with the perfection of this its idea, is plain in that it does not conceive, that any understanding hath, or can have a more complete or perfect idea of that thing it signifies by the word *triangle,* supposing it to exist, than itself has in that complex idea of three sides, and three angles; in which is contained all that is, or can be essential to it, or necessary to complete it, wherever or however it exists. But in our ideas of *substances,* it is otherwise. For there desiring to copy things as they really do exist; and to represent to ourselves that constitution on which all their properties depend, we perceive our ideas attain not that perfection we intend: we find they still want something we should be glad were in them;

and so are all *inadequate*. But *mixed modes* and *relations*, being archetypes without patterns, and so having nothing to represent but themselves, cannot but be adequate, everything being so to itself. He that at first put together the idea of danger perceived, absence of disorder from fear, sedate consideration of what was justly to be done, and executing of that without disturbance, or being deterred by the danger of it, had certainly in his mind that complex idea made up of that combination, and intending it to be nothing else, but what it is; nor to have in it any other simple ideas, but what it hath, it could not also but be an *adequate* idea: and laying this up in his memory, with the name *courage* annexed to it, to signify it to others, and denominate from thence any action he should observe to agree with it, had thereby a standard to measure and denominate actions by, as they agreed to it. This idea thus made, and laid up for a pattern, must necessarily be *adequate*, being referred to nothing else but itself, nor made by any other original, but the good-liking and will of him that first made this combination.

§4. Indeed, another coming after, and in conversation learning from him the word *courage*, may make an idea, to *Modes in reference to settled names, may be inadequate* which he gives that name *courage*, different from what the first author applied it to, and has in his mind, when he uses it. And in this case, if he designs, that his idea in thinking, should be conformable to the other's idea, as the name he uses in speaking is conformable in sound to his, from whom he learned it, his idea may be very wrong and *inadequate*. Because in this case, making the other man's idea the pattern of his idea in thinking, as the other man's word, or sound, is the pattern of his in speaking, his idea is so far defective and *inadequate*, as it is distant from the archetype and pattern he refers it to, and intends to express and signify by the name he uses for it; which name he would have to be a sign of the other man's idea, (to which, in its proper use, it is primarily annexed,) and of his own, as agreeing to it: to which, if his own does not exactly correspond, it is faulty and inadequate.

§5. Therefore these *complex ideas of modes*, when they are referred by the mind, and intended to correspond to the ideas in the mind of some other intelligent being, expressed by the names we apply to them, they *may be* very deficient, wrong, and *inadequate*. Because they agree not to that, which the mind designs to be their archetype and pattern: in which respect only, any idea of *modes* can be wrong, imperfect, or *inadequate*. And on this account, our ideas of *mixed modes* are the most liable to be faulty of any other; but this refers more to proper speaking, than knowing right.

Ideas of substances, as referred to real essences, not adequate

§6. *Thirdly*, what *ideas we have of substances*, I have above showed: now, those ideas have in the mind a double reference: 1. Sometimes they are referred to a supposed real essence of each species of things. 2. Sometimes they are only designed to be pictures and representations in the mind of things that do exist by ideas of those qualities that are discoverable in them. In both which ways, these copies of those originals and archetypes, *are* imperfect and *inadequate*.

First, it is usual for men to make the names of substances, stand for things, as supposed to have certain real essences, whereby they are of this or that species: and names standing for nothing but the ideas that are in men's minds, they must consequently refer their ideas to such real essences, as to their archetypes. That men (especially such as have been bred up in the learning taught in this part of the world) do suppose certain specific essences of substances, which each individual, in its several kinds, is made conformable to, and partakes of, is so far from needing proof, that it will be thought strange, if anyone should do otherwise. And thus they ordinarily apply the specific names, they rank particular substances under, to things, as distinguished by such specific real essences. Who is there almost, who would not take it amiss, if it should be doubted, whether he called himself man, with any other meaning, than as having the real essence of a man? And yet if you demand, what those real essences are, 'tis plain men are ignorant, and know them not. From whence it follows, that the ideas they have in their minds, being referred to real essences, as to archetypes which are unknown, must be so far from being *adequate*, that they cannot be supposed to be any representation of them at all. The complex ideas we have of substances, are, as it has been shown, certain collections of simple ideas that have been observed or supposed constantly to exist together. But such a complex idea cannot be the real essence of any substance; for then the properties we discover in that body, would depend on that complex idea, and be deducible from it, and their necessary connexion with it be known; as all properties of a triangle depend on, and as far as they are discoverable, are deducible from the complex idea of three lines, including a space. But it is plain, that in our complex ideas of substances, are not contained such ideas, on which all the other qualities, that are to be found in them, do depend. The common idea men have of *iron*, is a body of a certain colour, weight, and hardness; and a property that they look on as belonging to it, is malleableness. But yet this property has no necessary connexion with that complex idea, or any part of it: and there is no more reason to think, that malleableness depends on that colour, weight, and hardness, than that that colour, or that weight depends on its malleableness. And yet, though we know nothing of these real essences, there is nothing more ordinary, than that men should attribute the sorts of things to such essences. The particular parcel of matter, which makes the ring I have on my finger, is forwardly, by most men, supposed to have a real essence, whereby it is *gold*; and from whence those qualities flow, which I find in it, *viz.* its peculiar colour, weight, hardness, fusibility, fixedness, and change of colour upon a slight touch of mercury, *etc.* This essence, from which all these properties flow, when I inquire into it, and search after it, I plainly perceive I cannot discover: the furthest I can go, is only to presume, that it being nothing but body, its real essence, or internal constitution, on which these qualities depend, can be nothing but the figure, size, and connexion of its solid parts; of neither of which, I having any distinct perception at all, I can have no idea of its essence, which is the cause that it has that particular shining yellowness; a greater weight than anything I know of the same bulk, and a fitness to have its colour changed by the touch of quicksilver. If anyone will say, that the real essence, and internal constitution, on which these properties depend, is not the figure, size, and arrangement or connexion of its solid parts, but something else, called its particular *form*; I am further from having any idea of its real essence, than I was before; for I have an idea of figure, size, and situation of solid parts in general, though I have none of the particular figure, size, or putting together of parts, whereby the qualities above-mentioned are produced; which qualities I find in that particular parcel of matter that is on my finger, and not in another parcel of matter, with which I cut the pen I write with. But when I am told, that something besides the figure, size, and posture of the solid parts of that body, is its essence, something called *substantial form*; of that, I confess, I have no idea at all, but only of the sound *form*; which is far enough from an idea of its real essence, or constitution. The like ignorance as I have of the real essence of this particular substance, I have also of the real essence of all other natural ones: of which essences, I confess, I have no distinct ideas at all; and I am apt to suppose others, when they examine their own knowledge, will find in themselves, in this one point, the same sort of ignorance.

§7. Now then, when men apply to this particular parcel of matter on my finger, a general name already in use, and denominate it *gold*, do they not ordinarily, or are they not understood to give it that name as belonging to a particular species of bodies, having a real internal essence; by having of which essence, this particular substance comes to be of that species, and to be called by that name? If it be so, as it is plain it is, the name, by which things are marked, as having that essence, must be referred primarily to that essence; and consequently the idea to which that name is given, must be referred also to that essence, and be intended to represent it. Which essence, since they, who so use the names, know not, their *ideas of substances* must be *all inadequate* in that respect, as not containing in them that real essence which the mind intends they should.

Ideas of substances, §8. *Secondly,* those who neglecting
as collections of their that useless supposition of unknown real
qualities, are all essences, whereby they are distinguished,
inadequate endeavour to copy the substances that
exist in the world, by putting together the ideas of those sensible qualities which are found co-existing in them, though they come much nearer a likeness of them, than those who imagine they know not what real specific essences: yet they arrive not at perfectly adequate ideas of those substances they would thus copy into their minds; nor do those copies exactly and fully contain all that is to be found in their archetypes. Because those qualities, and powers of substances, whereof we make their complex ideas, are so many and various, that no man's complex idea contains them all. That our abstract ideas of substances, do not contain in them all the simple ideas that are united in the things themselves, is evident, in that men do rarely put into their complex idea of any substance, all the simple ideas they do know to exist in it. Because endeavouring to make the signification of their specific names as clear, and as little cumbersome

as they can, they make their specific ideas of the sorts of substances, for the most part, of a few of those simple ideas which are to be found in them: But these having no original precedency, or right to be put in, and make the specific idea more than others that are left out, 'tis plain, that both these ways, *our ideas of substances* are deficient and *inadequate*. The simple ideas, whereof we make our complex ones of substances, are all of them (bating only the figure and bulk of some sorts) powers, which being relations to other substances, we can never be sure that we know all the powers that are in any one body, till we have tried what changes it is fitted to give to, or receive from other substances, in their several ways of application: which being impossible to be tried upon any one body, much less upon all, it is impossible we should have adequate ideas of any substance, made up of a collection of all its properties.

§9. Whosoever first light on a parcel of that sort of substance we denote by the word *gold*, could not rationally take the bulk and figure he observed in that lump, to depend on its real essence or internal constitution. Therefore those never went into his idea of that species of body; but its peculiar colour, perhaps, and weight, were the first he abstracted from it, to make the complex idea of that species. Which both are but powers; the one to affect our eyes after such a manner, and to produce in us that idea we call yellow; and the other to force upwards any other body of equal bulk, they being put into a pair of equal scales, one against another. Another, perhaps, added to these, the ideas of fusibility and fixedness, two other passive powers, in relation to the operation of fire upon it; another, its ductility and solubility in *aqua regia*; two other powers, relating to the operation of other bodies, in changing its outward figure or separation of it into insensible parts. These, or part of these, put together, usually make the complex idea in men's minds, of that sort of body we call *gold*.

§10. But no one, who hath considered the properties of bodies in general, or this sort in particular, can doubt, that this, called *gold*, has infinite other properties, not contained in that complex idea. Some, who have examined this species more accurately, could, I believe, enumerate ten times as many properties in *gold*, all of them as inseparable from its internal constitution, as its colour, or weight: and 'tis probable, if anyone knew all the properties that are by divers men known of this metal, there would be an hundred times as many ideas go to the complex idea of *gold*, as any one man yet has in his; and yet, perhaps, that not be the thousandth part of what is to be discovered in it. The changes that that one body is apt to receive, and make in other bodies, upon a due application, exceeding far, not only what we know, but what we are apt to imagine. Which will not appear so much a paradox to anyone, who will but consider how far men are yet from knowing all the properties of that one, no very compound figure, a *triangle*, though it be no small number, that are already by mathematicians discovered of it.

§11. So that *all our complex ideas of substances are* imperfect and *inadequate*. Which would be so also in mathematical figures, if we were to have our complex ideas of them, only by collecting their properties in reference to other figures. How uncertain and imperfect would our ideas be of an *ellipse*, if we had no other idea of it, but some few of its properties? Whereas having in our plain idea, the whole essence of that figure, we from thence discover those properties, and demonstratively see how they flow, and are inseparable from it.

§12. Thus the mind has three sorts of abstract ideas, or nominal essences:

First, simple ideas, which are ἔκτυπα, or *copies*; but yet certainly *adequate*. Because being intended to express nothing but the power in things to produce in the mind such a sensation, that sensation, when it is produced, cannot but be the effect of that power. So the paper I write on, having the power, in the light, (I speak according to the common notion of light,) to produce in me the sensation which I call white, it cannot but be the effect of such a power, in something without the mind, since the mind has not the power to produce any such idea in itself, and being meant for nothing else but the effect of such a power; that simple idea is real and *adequate*: the sensation of white, in my mind, being the effect of that power, which is in the paper to produce it, is perfectly *adequate* to that power; or else, that power would produce a different idea.

Simple ideas ἔκτυπα, and adequate

§13. *Secondly,* the *complex ideas of sub- stances, are ectypes, copies* too; but not per- fect ones, not *adequate*: which is very evident to the mind, in that it plainly perceives, that whatever collection of simple ideas it makes of any substance that exists, it cannot be sure, that it exactly

Ideas of substances are ἔκτυπα, inadequate

answers all that are in that substance: since not having tried all the operations of all other substances upon it, and found all the alterations it would receive from, or cause in other substances, it cannot have an exact *adequate* collection of all its active and passive capacities; and so *not* have an *adequate* complex idea of the powers of any substance existing, and its relations, which is that sort of complex idea of substances we have. And, after all, if we could have, and actually had, in our complex idea, an exact collection of all the secondary qualities or powers of any substance, we should not yet thereby have an idea of the essence of that thing. For since the powers or qualities, that are observable by us, are not the real essence of that substance, but depend on it, and flow from it, any collection whatsoever of these qualities, cannot be the real essence of that thing. Whereby it is plain, that our ideas of substances are not *adequate*; are not what the mind intends them to be. Besides, a man has no idea of substance in general, nor knows what substance is in itself.

Ideas of modes and relations, are archetypes, and cannot but be adequate

§14. Thirdly, *complex ideas of modes and relations, are* originals, and *archetypes*; are not copies, nor made after the pattern of any real existence, to which the mind intends them to be conformable, and exactly to answer. These being such collections of simple ideas, that the mind itself puts together, and such collections, that each of them contains in it precisely all that the mind intends it should, they are archetypes and essences of modes that may exist; and so are designed only for, and belong only to such modes, as when they do exist, have an exact conformity with those complex ideas. The ideas therefore of modes and relations, cannot but be *adequate*.

Of True and False Ideas

§1. Though truth and falsehood belong, in propriety of speech, only to propositions; yet ideas are oftentimes termed *true or false*, (as what words are there, that are not used with great latitude, and with some deviation from their strict and proper significations?) Though, I think, that when ideas themselves are termed true or false, there is still some secret or tacit proposition, which is the foundation of that denomination: as we shall see, if we examine the particular occasions, wherein they come to be called true or false. In all which, we shall find some kind of affirmation, or negation, which is the reason of that denomination. For our ideas, being nothing but bare appearances or perceptions in our minds, cannot properly and simply in themselves be said to be *true* or *false*, no more than a single name of anything can be said to be *true* or *false*.

Truth and falsehood properly belong to propositions

§2. Indeed, both ideas and words, *may* be said to be *true in a metaphysical sense* of the word truth, as all other things, that any way exist, are said to be true; *i.e.* really to be such as they exist. Though in things called *true*, even in that sense, there is, perhaps, a secret reference to our ideas, looked upon as the standards of that truth, which

Metaphysical truth contains a tacit proposition

amounts to a mental proposition, though it be usually not taken notice of.

No idea, as an appearance in the mind, true or false §3. But 'tis not in that metaphysical sense of truth, which we inquire here, when we examine, whether our ideas are capable of being *true* or *false*; but in the more ordinary acceptation of those words: and so I say, that the ideas in our minds, being only so many perceptions, or appearances there, none of them are *false*. The idea of a centaur having no more falsehood in it, when it appears in our minds, than the name centaur has falsehood in it, when it is pronounced by our mouths, or written on paper. For truth or falsehood, lying always in some affirmation, or negation, mental or verbal, our ideas are *not capable*, any of them, *of being false*, till the mind passes some judgement on them; that is, affirms or denies something of them.

Ideas referred to anything, may be true or false §4. Whenever the mind refers any of its ideas to anything extraneous to them, they are then *capable to be called true or false*. Because the mind in such a reference, makes a tacit supposition of their conformity to that thing: which supposition, as it happens to be *true* or *false*; so the ideas themselves come to be denominated. The most usual cases wherein this happens, are these following:

Other men's ideas, real existence, and supposed real essences, are what men usually refer their ideas to §5. *First*, when the mind supposes any idea it has, *conformable to* that in *other men's* minds, called by the same common name; *v.g.* when the mind intends or judges its ideas of *justice*, *temperance*, *religion*, to be the same, with what other men give those names to.

Secondly, when the mind supposes any idea it has in

itself, to be *conformable to some real existence*. Thus the two ideas, of a man, and a centaur, supposed to be the ideas of real substances, are the one *true*, and the other *false*; the one having a conformity to what has really existed; the other not.

Thirdly, when the mind *refers* any of its *ideas to* that *real* constitution, and *essence* of anything, whereon all its properties depend: and thus the greatest part, if not all our ideas of substances, are *false*.

§6. These suppositions, the mind is very apt tacitly to make concerning its own ideas. *The cause of such references* But yet, if we will examine it, we shall find it is chiefly, if not only, concerning its abstract complex ideas. For the natural tendency of the mind being towards knowledge; and finding that, if it should proceed by, and dwell upon only particular things, its progress would be very slow, and its work endless: Therefore to shorten its way to knowledge, and make each perception the more comprehensive; the first thing it does, as the foundation of the easier enlarging its knowledge, either by contemplation of the things themselves, that it would know or conference with others about them, is to bind them into bundles, and rank them so into sorts, that what knowledge it gets of any of them, it may thereby with assurance extend to all of that sort; and so advance by larger steps in that, which is its great business, knowledge. This, as I have elsewhere showed, is the reason why we collect things under comprehensive ideas, with names annexed to them, into *genera* and *species*, *i.e.* into kinds and sorts.

§7. If therefore we will warily attend to the motions of the mind, and observe what course it usually takes in its way to knowledge, we shall, I think, find, that the mind having got any idea, which it thinks it may have use of, either in contemplation or discourse, the first thing it does, is to abstract it, and then get a name to it; and so lay it up in its storehouse, the memory, as containing the essence of a sort of things, of which that name is always to be the mark. Hence it is, that we may often observe, that when anyone sees a new thing of a kind that he knows not, he presently asks what it is, meaning by that inquiry, nothing but the name. As if the name carried with it the knowledge of the species, or the essence of it, whereof it is indeed used as the mark, and is generally supposed annexed to it.

§8. But this abstract idea being something in the mind between the thing that exists, and the name that is given to it; it is in our ideas, that both the rightness of our knowledge, and the propriety or intelligibleness of our speaking, consists. And hence it is, that men are so forward to suppose, that the abstract ideas they have in their minds, are such as agree to the things existing without them, to which they are referred; and are the same also, to which the names they give them, do, by the use and propriety of that language belong. For without this *double conformity of* their *ideas*, they find they should both think amiss of things in themselves, and talk of them unintelligibly to others.

Simple ideas may be false, in reference to others of the same name, but are least liable to be so

§9. *First* then, I say, that *when the truth of our ideas is judged of, by the conformity they have to the ideas which other men have, and commonly signify by the same name, they may be any of them false.* But yet *simple ideas* are *least* of all *liable to be so mistaken.* Because a man by his senses, and every day's observation, may easily satisfy himself what the simple ideas are, which their several names that are in common use stand for, they being but few in number, and such, as if he doubts or mistakes in, he may easily rectify by the objects they are to be found in. Therefore it is seldom, that anyone mistakes in his names of simple ideas; or applies the name *red*, to the idea of green; or the name sweet, to the idea bitter: much less are men apt to confound the names of ideas, belonging to different senses; and call a colour, by the name of a taste, *etc.* whereby it is evident, that the simple ideas they call by any name, are commonly the same that others have and mean, when they use the same names.

§10. *Complex ideas are much more liable to be false in this respect; and the complex ideas of mixed modes, much more than those of substances*: because in substances, (especially those which the common and unborrowed names of any language are applied to) some remarkable sensible qualities, serving ordinarily to distinguish one sort from another, easily preserve those, who take any care in the use of their words, from applying them to sorts of substances to which they do not at all belong. But in mixed modes, we are much more uncertain, it being not so easy to determine of several actions, whether they are to be called *justice*, or *cruelty*; *liberality*, or *prodigality*. And so in referring our ideas to those of other men, called by the same names, ours may be *false*; and the idea in our minds, which we express by the word *justice*, may, perhaps, be that which ought to have another name.

Ideas of mixed modes most liable to be false in this sense

John Locke

Or at least to be thought false §11. But whether or no our ideas of mixed modes are more liable than any sort, to be different from those of other men, which are marked by the same names: this at least is certain, that *this sort of falsehood is much more familiarly attributed to our ideas of mixed modes, than to any other*. When a man is thought to have a false idea of *justice*, or *gratitude*, or *glory*, it is for no other reason, but that his agrees not with the ideas which each of those names are the signs of in other men.

And why §12. *The reason whereof* seems to me to be this, that the abstract ideas of mixed modes, being men's voluntary combinations of such a precise collection of simple ideas; and so the essence of each species being made by men alone, whereof we have no other sensible standard existing anywhere, but the name itself, or the definition of that name: we have nothing else to refer these our ideas of mixed modes to, as a standard, to which we would conform them, but the ideas of those, who are thought to use those names in their most proper significations; and so, as our ideas conform, or differ from them, they pass for true or false. And thus much concerning the *truth* and *falsehood* of our ideas, in reference to their names.

As referred to real existences, none of our ideas can be false, but those of substances §13. *Secondly*, as to the *truth and falsehood of our ideas, in reference* to the *real existence* of things, when that is made the standard of their truth, none of them can be termed false, but only our complex ideas of substances.

§14. *First*, our simple ideas being barely such perceptions, as God has fitted us to receive, and given power to exter-

nal objects to produce in us by established laws and ways, suitable to his wisdom and goodness, though incomprehensible to us, their truth consists in nothing else but in such appearances as are produced in us, and must be suitable to those powers he has placed in external objects, or else they could not be produced in us: and thus answering those powers, they are what they should be, *true* ideas. Nor do they become liable to any impu- tation of *falsehood*, if the mind (as in most men I believe it does) judges these ideas to be in the things themselves. For God, in his wisdom, having set them as marks of distinction in things, whereby we may be able to discern one thing from another, and so choose any of them for our uses, as we have occasion, it alters not the nature of our simple idea, whether we think, that the idea of blue, be in the violet itself, or in our mind only; and only the power of producing it by the texture of its parts, reflecting the particles of light, after a certain manner, to be in the violet itself. For that texture in the object, by a regular and constant operation, producing the same idea of blue in us, it serves us to distinguish, by our eyes, that from any other thing, whether that distinguishing mark, as it is really in the *violet*, be only a peculiar texture of parts, or else that very colour, the idea whereof (which is in us) is the exact resemblance. And it is equally from that appearance to be denominated *blue*, whether it be that real colour, or only a peculiar texture in it, that causes in us that idea: since the name *blue* notes properly nothing, but that mark of distinction that is in a *violet*, discernible only by our eyes, whatever it consists in, that being beyond our capacities distinctly to know, and, perhaps, would be of less use to us, if we had faculties to discern.

Though one man's idea of   §15. Neither would it carry any impu-
blue should be different   tation of *falsehood* to our simple ideas,
from another's   *if* by the different structure of our organs, it were so ordered, that *the same object should produce in several men's minds different ideas* at the same time; *v.g.* if the idea that a *violet* produced in one man's mind by his eyes, were the same that a *marigold* produced in another man's, and *vice versâ*. For since this could never be known; because one man's mind could not pass into another man's body, to perceive what appearances were produced by those organs; neither the ideas hereby, nor the names would be at all confounded, or any *falsehood* be in either. For all things that had the texture of a *violet*, producing constantly the idea which he called *blue*; and those which had the texture of a *marigold*, producing constantly the idea which he as constantly called *yellow*, whatever those appearances were in his mind, he would be able as regularly to distinguish things for his use by those appearances, and understand and signify those distinctions, marked by the names *blue* and *yellow*, as if the appearances, or ideas in his mind, received from those two flowers, were exactly the same with the ideas in other men's minds. I am nevertheless very apt to think, that the sensible ideas produced by any object in different men's minds, are most commonly very near and undiscernibly alike. For which opinion, I think, there

might be many reasons offered: but that being besides my present business, I shall not trouble my reader with them; but only mind him, that the contrary supposition, if it could be proved, is of little use, either for the improvement of our knowledge, or conveniency of life; and so we need not trouble ourselves to examine it.

§16. From what has been said concerning our simple ideas, I think it evident, that our *simple ideas* can *none of them* be *false, in respect of things* existing without us. For the truth of these appearances, or perceptions in our minds, consisting, as has been said, only in their being answerable to the powers in external objects, to produce by our senses such appearances in us, and each of them being in the mind, such as it is, suitable to the power that produced it, and which alone it represents, it cannot upon that account, or as referred to such a pattern, be *false*. *Blue* or *yellow*, *bitter* or *sweet*, can never be false ideas, these perceptions in the mind are just such as they are there, answering the powers appointed by God to produce them; and so are truly what they are, and are intended to be. Indeed the names may be misapplied; but that in this respect, makes no falsehood in the ideas: as if a man ignorant in the English tongue, should call *purple*, *scarlet*.

First, simple ideas in this sense not false, and why

§17. *Secondly, neither can* our *complex ideas of modes, in reference to the essence of anything really existing, be false.* Because whatever complex idea I have of any mode, it hath no reference to any pattern existing, and made by nature: it is not supposed to contain in it any other ideas, than

Secondly, modes not false

what it hath; nor to represent anything, but such a complication of ideas as it does. Thus when I have the idea of such an action of a man, who forbears to afford himself such meat, drink, and clothing, and other conveniencies of life, as his riches and estate will be sufficient to supply, and his station requires, I have no *false* idea; but such an one as represents an action, either as I find or imagine it; and so is capable of neither *truth*, or *falsehood*. But when I give the name *frugality*, or *virtue*, to this action, then it may be called a *false* idea, if thereby it be supposed to agree with that idea, to which, in propriety of speech, the name of *frugality* doth belong; or to be conformable to that law, which is the standard of virtue and vice.

Thirdly, ideas of §18. *Thirdly,* our complex *ideas of sub-*
substances when false *stances, being all referred to patterns in things themselves, may be false.* That they are all *false*, when looked upon as the representations of the unknown essences of things, is so evident, that there needs nothing to be said of it. I shall therefore pass over that chimerical supposition, and consider them as collections of simple ideas in the mind, taken from combinations of simple ideas existing together constantly in things, of which patterns they are the supposed copies: and in this reference of them, to the existence of things, they *are false ideas.* 1. *When* they put together simple ideas, which in the real existence of things have no union; as when to the shape and size that exist together in a horse, is joined, in the same complex idea, the power of barking like dog: which three ideas, however put together into one in the mind, were never united in nature; and this therefore

may be called a *false* idea of an horse. 2. Ideas of substances are, in this respect, also *false*, when from any collection of simple ideas that do always exist together, there is separated, by a direct negation, any other simple idea which is constantly joined with them. Thus if to extension, solidity, fusibility, the peculiar weightiness, and yellow colour of gold, anyone join in his thoughts the negation of a greater degree of fixedness than is in lead or copper, he may be said to have a false complex idea, as well as when he joins to those other simple ones, the idea of perfect absolute fixedness. For either way, the complex idea of gold being made up of such simple ones, as have no union in nature, may be termed false. But if he leave out of this his complex idea, that of fixedness quite, without either actually joining to, or separating of it from the rest in his mind, it is, I think, to be looked on, as an inadequate and imperfect idea, rather than a *false* one; since though it contains not all the simple ideas that are united in nature, yet it puts none together but what do really exist together.

§19. Though in compliance with the ordinary way of speaking, I have showed in what sense, and upon what ground our ideas may be sometimes called *true*, or *false*; *Truth or falsehood always supposes affirmation or negation* yet if we will look a little nearer into the matter in all cases, where any idea is called *true*, or *false*, it is from some judgement that the mind makes, or is supposed to make, that is *true* or *false*. For *truth or falsehood*, being *never without some affirmation, or negation*, express or tacit, it is not to be found, but where signs are joined or separated, according to the agreement, or disagreement of the things they stand for. The signs we chiefly use, are either ideas, or words, wherewith we make either mental or verbal propositions. *Truth* lies in so joining or separating these representatives, as the things they stand for, do in themselves, agree or disagree; and *falsehood* in the contrary, as shall be more fully showed hereafter.

Ideas in themselves   §20. Any idea then which we have in *neither true nor false*   our minds, whether conformable or not to the existence of things, or to any ideas in the minds of other men, cannot properly for this alone be called *false*. For these representations, if they have nothing in them, but what is really existing in things without, cannot be thought *false*, being exact representations of something: nor yet if they have anything in them, differing from the reality of things, can they properly be said to be false representations, or ideas of things, they do not represent. But the mistake and *falsehood* is,

But are false, first,   §21. *First, when the mind* having any *when judged agreeable*   idea, it *judges* and concludes *it the same to another man's idea*   *that is in other men's minds, signified by without being so*   *the same name*; or that it is conformable to the ordinary received signification or definition of that word, when indeed it is not: which is the most usual mistake in mixed modes, though other ideas also are liable to it.

Secondly, when judged   §22. *Secondly,* when it having a com- *to agree to real existence,*   plex idea made up of such a collection of *when they do not*   simple ones, as nature never puts to- gether, *it judges it to agree to a species of creatures really existing*; as when it joins the weight of tin, to the colour, fusibility, and fixedness of gold.

§23. *Thirdly*, when in its complex idea, *Thirdly, when judged*
it has united a certain number of simple *adequate, without*
ideas, that do really exist together in *being so*
some sorts of creatures, but has also left out others, as
much inseparable, *it judges this to be a perfect complete
idea, of a sort of things which really it is not*; *v.g.* having
joined the ideas of substance, yellow, malleable, most
heavy, and fusible, it takes that complex idea to be the
complete idea of gold, when yet its peculiar fixedness
and solubility in *aqua regia*, are as inseparable from those
other ideas or qualities of that body, as they are one
from another.

§24. *Fourthly*, the mistake is yet *Fourthly, when*
greater, *when I judge, that this complex* *judged to represent the*
idea contains in it the real essence of any *real essence*
body existing; when at least it contains but some few of
those properties which flow from its real essence and
constitution. I say, only some few of those properties;
for those properties consisting mostly in the active and
passive powers, it has, in reference to other things, all
that are vulgarly known of any one body, and of which
the complex idea of that kind of things is usually made,
are but a very few, in comparison of what a man, that
has several ways tried and examined it, knows of that
one sort of things; and all that the most expert man
knows, are but few, in comparison of what are really
in that body, and depend on its internal or essential
constitution. The essence of a triangle, lies in a very little
compass, consists in a very few ideas; three lines including
a space, make up that essence: but the properties that
flow from this essence, are more than can be easily

known, or enumerated. So I imagine it is in substances, their real essences lie in a little compass; though the properties flowing from that internal constitution, are endless.

Ideas when false §25. To conclude, a man having no notion of anything without him, but by the idea he has of it in his mind, (which idea he has a power to call by what name he pleases) he may, indeed, make an idea neither answering the reality of things, nor agreeing to the ideas commonly signified by other people's words; but cannot make a wrong or *false* idea of a thing which is no otherwise known to him, but by the idea he has of it. *V.g.* When I frame an idea of the legs, arms, and body of a man, and join to this a horse's head and neck, I do not make a *false* idea of anything; because it represents nothing without me. But when I call it a *man*, or *Tartar*, and imagine it either to represent some real being without me, or to be the same idea that others call by the same name; in either of these cases, I may err. And upon this account it is, that it comes to be termed a *false* idea; though, indeed, the *falsehood* lies not in the idea, but in that tacit mental proposition, wherein a conformity and resemblance is attributed to it, which it has not. But yet, if having framed such an idea in my mind, without thinking, either that existence, or the name *man* or *Tartar*, belongs to it, I will call it *man* or *Tartar*, I may be justly thought fantastical in the naming; but not erroneous in my judgement; nor the idea any way *false*.

More properly to be §26. Upon the whole matter, I think, *called right or wrong* that our ideas, as they are considered by the mind, either in reference to the proper signification of their names, or in reference to the reality of things, *may* very fitly *be called right or wrong ideas*, according as they agree or disagree to those patterns to which they are referred. But if anyone had rather call them *true* or *false*, 'tis fit he use a liberty, which everyone has, to call things by those names he thinks best; though in propriety of speech, *truth* or *falsehood*, will, I think, scarce agree to them, but as they, some way or other, virtually contain in them some mental proposition. The ideas that are in a man's mind, simply considered, cannot be wrong, unless complex ones, wherein inconsistent parts are jumbled together. All other ideas are in themselves right; and the knowledge about them, right and true knowledge: but when we come to refer them to any thing, as to their patterns and archetypes, then they are capable of being wrong, as far as they disagree with such archetypes.

Of Words

Of Words or Language in General

Man fitted to form §1. God having designed man for a soci-
articulate sounds able creature, made him not only with an
inclination, and under a necessity to have fellowship with
those of his own kind; but furnished him also with
language, which was to be the great instrument, and
common tie of society. *Man* therefore had by nature his
organs so fashioned, as to be *fit to frame articulate sounds*,
which we call words. But this was not enough to produce
language; for parrots, and several other birds, will be
taught to make articulate sounds distinct enough, which
yet, by no means, are capable of language.

To make them §2. Besides articulate sounds therefore, it
signs of ideas was further necessary, that he should be *able
to use these sounds, as signs of internal conceptions*; and to
make them stand as marks for the ideas within his own
mind, whereby they might be made known to others,
and the thoughts of men's minds be conveyed from one
to another.

To make §3. But neither was this sufficient to make
general signs words so useful as they ought to be. It is not
enough for the perfection of language, that sounds can be
made signs of ideas, unless those *signs* can be so made
use of, as *to comprehend several particular things*: for the

multiplication of words would have perplexed their use, had every particular thing need of a distinct name to be signified by. To remedy this inconvenience, language had yet a further improvement in the use of general terms, whereby one word was made to mark a multitude of particular existences: which advantageous use of sounds was obtained only by the difference of the ideas they were made signs of. Those names becoming general, which are made to stand for general ideas, and those remaining particular, where the ideas they are used for are particular.

§4. Besides these names which stand for ideas, there be other words which men make use of, not to signify any idea, but the want or absence of some ideas simple or complex, or all ideas together; such as are the *nihil* in Latin, and in English, *ignorance* and *barrenness*. All which negative or privative words, cannot be said properly to belong to, or signify no ideas: for then they would be perfectly insignificant sounds; but they relate to positive ideas, and signify their absence.

§5. It may also lead us a little towards the original of all our notions and knowledge, if we remark, how great a dependence our *words* have on common sensible ideas; and how those, which are made use of to stand for actions and notions quite removed from sense, *have their rise from thence, and from obvious sensible ideas are transferred to more abstruse significations*, and made to stand for ideas that come not under the cognizance of our senses; *v.g.* to *imagine, apprehend, comprehend, adhere, conceive, instil, disgust, disturbance, tranquillity*, etc. are all words taken from the operations of sensible things, and applied to

Words ultimately derived from such as signify sensible ideas

certain modes of thinking. *Spirit*, in its primary signification, is breath; *angel*, a messenger: and I doubt not, but if we could trace them to their sources, we should find, in all languages, the names, which stand for things that fall not under our senses, to have had their first rise from sensible ideas. By which we may give some kind of guess, what kind of notions they were, and whence derived, which filled their minds, who were the first beginners of languages; and how nature, even in the naming of things, unawares suggested to men the originals and principles of all their knowledge: whilst, to give names, that might make known to others any operations they felt in themselves, or any other ideas, that came not under their senses, they were fain to borrow words from ordinary known ideas of sensation, by that means to make others the more easily to conceive those operations they experimented in themselves, which made no outward sensible appearances; and then when they had got known and agreed names, to signify those internal operations of their own minds, they were sufficiently furnished to make known by words, all their other ideas; since they could consist of nothing, but either of outward sensible perceptions, or of the inward operations of their minds about them; we having, as has been proved, no ideas at all, but what originally come either from sensible objects without, or what we feel within ourselves, from the inward workings of our own spirits, which we are conscious to ourselves of within.

Distribution §6. But to understand better the use and force of language, as subservient to instruction and knowledge, it will be convenient to consider,

First, to what it is that names, in the use of language, are immediately applied.

Secondly, since all (except proper) names are general, and so stand not particularly for this or that single thing; but for sorts and ranks of things, it will be necessary to consider, in the next place, what the sorts and kinds, or, if you rather like the Latin names, *what the species and genera of things* are; wherein they consist; and how they come to be made. These being (as they ought) well looked into, we shall the better come to find the right use of words; the natural advantages and defects of language; and the remedies that ought to be used, to avoid the inconveniencies of obscurity or uncertainty in the signification of words, without which, it is impossible to discourse with any clearness, or order, concerning knowledge: which being conversant about propositions, and those most commonly universal ones, has greater connexion with words, than perhaps is suspected.

These considerations therefore, shall be the matter of the following chapters.

Of the Imperfection of Words

§1. From what has been said in the foregoing chapters, it is easy to perceive, what imperfection there is in language, and how the very nature of words, makes it almost unavoidable, for many of them to be doubtful and uncertain in their significations. To examine the perfection, or imperfection of words, it is necessary first to consider

Words are used for recording and communicating our thoughts

their use and end: for as they are more or less fitted to attain that, so are they more or less perfect. We have, in the former part of this discourse, often, upon occasion, mentioned *a double use of words*.

First, one for the recording of our own thoughts.

Secondly, the other for the communicating of our thoughts to others.

Any words will serve for recording §2. As to the first of these, *for the recording our own thoughts* for the help of our own memories, whereby, as it were, we talk to ourselves, any words will serve the turn. For since sounds are voluntary and indifferent signs of any ideas, a man may use what words he pleases, to signify his own ideas to himself: and there will be no imperfection in them, if he constantly use the same sign for the same idea: for then he cannot fail of having his meaning understood, wherein consists the right use and perfection of language.

Communication by words civil or philosophical §3. *Secondly*, As to *communication of words*, that too *has a double use*.

I. *Civil.*

II. *Philosophical.*

First, By their *civil use*, I mean such a communication of thoughts and ideas by words, as may serve for the upholding common conversation and commerce, about the ordinary affairs and conveniencies of civil life, in the societies of men one amongst another.

Secondly, by the *philosophical use* of words, I mean such an use of them, as may serve to convey the precise notions of things, and to express, in general propositions, certain and undoubted truths, which the mind may rest upon, and be satisfied with, in its search after true knowledge. These two uses are very distinct; and a great deal less exactness will serve in the one, than in the other, as we shall see in what follows.

§4. The chief end of language in communication being to be understood, words serve not well for that end, neither in civil, nor philosophical discourse, when *The imperfections of words is the doubtfulness of their signification* any word does not excite in the hearer, the same idea which it stands for in the mind of the speaker. Now since sounds have no natural connexion with our ideas, but have all their signification from the arbitrary imposition of men, the *doubtfulness* and uncertainty *of their signification*, which *is the imperfection* we here are speaking of, has its cause more in the ideas they stand for, than in any incapacity there is in one sound, more than in another, to signify any idea: for in that regard, they are all equally perfect.

That then which makes doubtfulness and uncertainty in the signification of some more than other words, is the difference of ideas they stand for.

§5. Words having naturally no signification, the idea which each stands for, must *Causes of their imperfection* be learned and retained by those, who would exchange thoughts, and hold intelligible discourse with others, in any language. But this is hardest to be done, where,

First, the ideas they stand for, are very complex, and made up of a great number of ideas put together.

Secondly, where the ideas they stand for, have no

certain connexion in nature; and so no settled standard, anywhere in nature existing, to rectify and adjust them by.

Thirdly, where the signification of the word is referred to a standard, which standard is not easy to be known.

Fourthly, where the signification of the word, and the real essence of the thing, are not exactly the same.

These are difficulties that attend the signification of several words that are intelligible. Those which are not intelligible at all, such as names standing for any simple ideas, which another has not organs or faculties to attain; as the names of colours to a blind man, or sounds to a deaf man, need not here be mentioned.

In all these cases, we shall find an imperfection in words; which I shall more at large explain, in their particular application to our several sorts of ideas: for if we examine them, we shall find, that the *names of mixed modes are most liable to doubtfulness and imperfection, for the two first of these reasons; and the names of substances chiefly for the two latter.*

The names of mixed modes doubtful. First, because the ideas they stand for, are so complex §6. *First*, the names of *mixed modes*, are many of them liable to great uncertainty and obscurity in their signification.

I. *Because of* that great *composition*, these complex ideas are often made up of. To make words serviceable to the end of communication, it is necessary, (as has been said) that they excite, in the hearer, exactly the same idea, they stand for in the mind of the speaker. Without this, men fill one another's heads with noise and sounds; but convey not thereby their thoughts, and lay not before one another their ideas, which is the end of discourse and language. But when a word stands for a very complex idea, that is compounded and decompounded, it is not easy for men to form and retain that idea so exactly, as to make the name in common use, stand for the same precise idea, without any the least variation. Hence it comes to pass, that men's names, of very compound ideas, such as for the most part are moral words, have seldom, in two different men, the same precise signification; since one man's complex idea seldom agrees with another's, and often differs from his own, from that which he had yesterday, or will have tomorrow.

§7. II. *Because the names of mixed modes,* Secondly, because for the most part, *want standards* in nature, they have no whereby men may rectify and adjust their standards significations; therefore they are very various and doubtful. They are assemblages of ideas put together at the pleasure of the mind, pursuing its own ends of discourse, and suited to its own notions; whereby it designs not to copy anything really existing, but to denominate and rank things, as they come to agree, with those archetypes or forms it has made. He that first brought the word *sham, wheedle,* or *banter* in use, put together, as he thought fit, those ideas he made it stand for: and as it is with any new names of modes, that are now brought into any language; so was it with the old ones, when they were first made use of. Names therefore, that stand for collections of ideas, which the mind makes at pleasure, must needs be of doubtful signification, when such collections are nowhere to be found constantly united in nature, nor any patterns to be shown whereby men may adjust them. What the word *murder*, or *sacrilege*, *etc.* signifies, can never be known from things themselves: there be many of the parts of those complex ideas, which are not visible in the action itself, the intention of the mind, or the relation of holy things, which make a part of *murder*, or *sacrilege*, have no necessary connexion with the outward and visible action of him that commits either: and the pulling the trigger of the gun, with which the murder is committed, and is all the action, that, perhaps, is visible, has no natural connexion with those other ideas, that make up the complex one, named *murder*. They have their union and combination only from the understanding which unites them under one name: but uniting them without any rule, or pattern, it cannot be but that the signification of the name, that stands for such voluntary collections, should be often various in the minds of different men, who have scarce any standing rule to regulate themselves, and their notions by, in such arbitrary ideas.

Propriety not a sufficient remedy §8. 'Tis true, *common use*, that is the rule of propriety, may be supposed here to afford some aid, to settle the signification of language; and it cannot be denied, but that in some measure it does. Common use *regulates the meaning of words* pretty well for common conversation; but nobody having an authority to establish the precise signification of words, nor determine to what ideas anyone shall annex them, common use is not sufficient to adjust them to philosophical discourses; there being scarce any name, of any very complex idea, (to say nothing of others,) which, in common use, has not a great latitude, and which keeping within the bounds of propriety, may not be made the sign of far different ideas. Besides the rule and measure of propriety itself being nowhere established, it is often matter of dispute, whether this or that way of using a word, be propriety of speech, or no. From all which, it is evident, that the names of such kind of very complex ideas, are naturally liable to this imperfection, to be of doubtful and uncertain signification; and even in men, that have a mind to understand one another, do not always stand for the same idea in speaker and hearer. Though the names *glory* and *gratitude* be the same in every man's mouth, through a whole country, yet the complex collective idea, which everyone thinks on, or intends by that name, is apparently very different in men using the same language.

§9. *The way* also *wherein the names of mixed modes are ordinarily learned, does not a little contribute to the doubtfulness of their signification.* For if we will observe how *The way of learning these names contributes also to their doubtfulness* children learn languages, we shall find, that to make them understand what the names of simple ideas, or substances, stand for, people ordinarily show them the thing, whereof they would have them have the idea; and then repeat to them the name that stands for it, as *white, sweet, milk, sugar, cat, dog*. But as for mixed modes, especially the most material of them, moral words, the sounds are usually learned first, and then to know what complex ideas they stand for, they are either beholden to the explication of others, or (which happens for the most part) are left to their own observation and industry;

which being little laid out in the search of the true and precise meaning of names, these moral words are, in most men's mouths, little more than bare sounds; or when they have any, 'tis for the most part but a very loose and undetermined, and consequently obscure and confused signification. And even those themselves, who have with more attention settled their notions, do yet hardly avoid the inconvenience, to have them stand for complex ideas, different from those which other, even intelligent and studious men, make them the signs of. Where shall one find any, either *controversial debate*, or *familiar discourse*, concerning *honour*, *faith*, *grace*, *religion*, *church*, etc. wherein it is not easy to observe the different notions men have of them; which is nothing but this, that they are not agreed in the signification of those words; nor have in their minds the same complex ideas which they make them stand for: and so all the contests that follow thereupon, are only about the meaning of a sound. And hence we see, that in the interpretation of laws, whether divine, or human, there is no end; comments beget comments, and explications make new matter for explications: and of limiting, distinguishing, varying the signification of these moral words, there is no end. These ideas of men's making, are, by men still having the same power, multiplied *in infinitum*. Many a man, who was pretty well satisfied of the meaning of a text of Scripture, or clause in the code, at first reading, has by consulting commentators, quite lost the sense of it, and, by those elucidations, given rise or increase to his doubts, and drawn obscurity upon the place. I say not this, that I think commentaries needless; but to show

how uncertain the names of mixed modes naturally are, even in the mouths of those, who had both the intention and the faculty of speaking as clearly, as language was capable to express their thoughts.

§10. What obscurity this has un- *Hence unavoidable* avoidably brought upon the writings of *obscurity in ancient* men, who have lived in remote ages, and *authors* different countries, it will be needless to take notice. Since the numerous volumes of learned men, employing their thoughts that way, are proofs more than enough, to show what attention, study, sagacity, and reasoning is required, to find out the true meaning *of ancient authors.* But there being no writings we have any great concernment to be very solicitous about the meaning of, but those that contain either truths we are required to believe, or laws we are to obey, and draw inconveniences on us, when we mistake or transgress, we may be less anxious about the sense of other authors; who writing but their own opinions, we are under no greater necessity to know them, than they to know ours. Our good or evil depending not on their decrees, we may safely be ignorant of their notions: and therefore in the reading of them, if they do not use their words with a due clearness and perspicuity, we may lay them aside, and without any injury done them, resolve thus with ourselves,

Si non vis intelligi, debes negligi.

['If you don't want to be understood, you should be discounted']

§11. If the signification of the names of mixed modes are uncertain, because there be no real standards existing in nature, to which those ideas are referred, and by which they may be adjusted, the *names of substances are of a doubtful signification,* for a contrary reason, *viz. because the ideas,* they stand for, are supposed conformable to the reality of things, and are *referred to standards* made by nature. In our ideas of substances we have not the liberty as in mixed modes, to frame what combinations we think fit, to be the characteristical notes, to rank and denominate things by. In these we must follow nature, suit our complex ideas to real existences, and regulate the signification of their names by the things themselves, if we will have our names to be the signs of them, and stand for them. Here, 'tis true, we have patterns to follow; but patterns, that will make the signification of their names very uncertain: for names must be of a very unsteady and various meaning, if the ideas they stand for, be referred to standards without us, *that either cannot be known at all, or can be known but imperfectly and uncertainly.*

Names of substances referred, first, to real essences that cannot be known

§12. The *names of substances have,* as has been showed, a double *reference* in their ordinary use.

First, sometimes they are made to stand for, and so their signification is supposed to agree to, *the real constitution of things,* from which all their properties flow, and in which they all centre. But this real constitution, or (as it is apt to be called) essence, being utterly unknown to us, any sound that is put to stand for it, must be very uncertain in its application; and it will be impossible to know, what things are, or ought to be called an *horse,* or *antimony,* when those words are put for real essences, that we have no ideas of at all. And therefore in this supposition, the names of substances being referred to standards that cannot be known, their significations can never be adjusted and established by those standards.

§13. *Secondly*, the *simple ideas* that are found to *co-exist in substances*, being that which their names immediately signify, *Secondly, to co-existing qualities, which are known but imperfectly* these, as united in the several sorts of things, *are* the proper *standards* to which their names are referred, and by which their significations may best be rectified. But neither will these archetypes so well serve to this purpose, as to leave these names, without very various and uncertain significations. Because these simple ideas that co-exist, and are united in the same subject, being very numerous, and having all an equal right to go into the complex specific idea, which the specific name is to stand for, men, though they propose to themselves the very same subject to consider, yet frame very different ideas about it; and so the name they use for it, unavoidably comes to have, in several men, very different significations. The simple qualities which make up the complex ideas, being most of them powers, in relation to changes, which they are apt to make in, or receive from other bodies, are almost infinite. He that shall but observe, what a great variety of alterations any one of the baser metals is apt to receive, from the different application only of fire; and how much a greater number of changes any of them will receive in the hands of a chemist, by the application of other bodies, will not think it strange, that I count the properties of any sort of bodies not easy to be collected, and completely known by the ways of inquiry, which our faculties are capable of. They being therefore at least so many, that no man can know the precise and definite number, they are differently discovered by different men, according to their various skill, attention, and ways of handling; who therefore cannot choose but have different ideas of the same substance, and therefore make the signification of its common name very various and uncertain. For the complex ideas of substances, being made up of such simple ones as are supposed to co-exist in nature, everyone has a right to put into his complex idea, those qualities he has found to be united together. For though in the substance *gold*, one satisfies himself with colour and weight, yet another thinks solubility in *aqua regia*, as necessary to be joined with that colour in his idea of gold, as anyone does its fusibility; solubility in *aqua regia*, being a quality as constantly joined with its colour and weight, as fusibility, or any other; others put in its ductility or fixedness, *etc.* as they have been taught by tradition, or experience. Who of all these, has established the right signification of the word *gold*? Or who shall be the judge to determine? Each has his standard in nature, which he appeals to, and with reason thinks he has the same right to put into his complex idea, signified by the word *gold*, those qualities, which upon trial he has found united; as another, who has not so well examined, has to leave them out; or a third, who has made other trials, has to put in others. For the union in nature of these qualities, being the true ground of their union in one complex idea, who can say, one of them has more reason to be put in, or left out, than another? From whence it will always unavoidably follow, that the complex ideas of substances, in men using the same name for them, will be very various; and so the significations of those names, very uncertain.

§14. Besides, there is scarce any particular thing existing, which, in some of its simple ideas, does not communicate with a greater, and in others with a less number of particular beings: who shall determine in this case, which are those that are to make up the precise collection, that is to be signified by the specific name; or can with any just authority prescribe, which obvious or common qualities are to be left out; or which more secret, or more particular, are to be put into the signification of the name of any substance? All *which* together, seldom or never fail to *produce* that various and *doubtful signification in the names of substances*, which causes such uncertainty, disputes, or mistakes, when we come to a philosophical use of them.

§15. 'Tis true, as *to civil and common conversation*, the general *names of substances*, regulated in their ordinary signification by some obvious qualities, (as *With this imperfection, they may serve for civil, but not well for philosophical use* by the shape and figure in things of known seminal propagation, and in other substances, for the most part by colour, joined with some other sensible qualities,) *do well enough*, to design the things men would be understood to speak of: and so they usually conceive well enough the substances meant by the word *gold*, or *apple*, to distinguish the one from the other. *But in philosophical inquiries and debates*, where general truths *are* to be established, and consequences drawn from positions laid down, there the precise signification of the names of substances will be found, not only *not* to be *well established*, but also very hard to be so. For example, he that shall make malleableness, or a certain degree of fixedness, a part of his complex idea of *gold*, may make propositions concerning gold, and draw consequences from them, that will truly and clearly follow from *gold*, taken in such a signification: But yet such as another man can never be forced to admit, nor be convinced of their truth, who makes not malleableness, or the same degree of fixedness, part of that complex idea, that the name *gold*, in his use of it, stands for.

Instance liquor   §16. This is a natural, and almost unavoidable imperfection in almost all the names of substances, in all languages whatsoever, which men will easily find, when once passing from confused or loose notions, they come to more strict and close inquiries. For then they will be convinced, how doubtful and obscure those words are in their signification, which in ordinary use appeared very clear and determined. I was once in a meeting of very learned and ingenious physicians, where by chance there arose a question, whether any liquor passed through the filaments of the nerves. The debate having been managed a good while, by variety of arguments on both sides, I (who had been used to suspect, that the greatest part of disputes were more about the signification of words, than a real difference in the conception of things) desired, that before they went any further on in this dispute, they would first examine, and establish amongst them, what the word *liquor* signified. They at first were a little surprised at the proposal; and had they been persons less ingenious, they might perhaps have taken it for a very frivolous or extravagant one: since there was no one there, that thought not himself to understand very perfectly, what the word *liquor* stood for; which, I think too, none of the most perplexed names of substances. However, they were pleased to comply with my motion, and upon examination found, that the signification of that word, was not so settled and certain, as they had all imagined; but that each of them made it a sign of a different complex idea. This made them perceive, that the main of their dispute was about the signification of that term; and that they differed very little in their opinions, concerning some fluid and subtle matter, passing through the conduits of the nerves; though it was not so easy to agree whether it was to be called *liquor*, or no, a thing which when each considered, he thought it not worth the contending about.

§17. How much this is the case in the great-   *Instance gold* est part of disputes, that men are engaged so hotly in, I shall, perhaps, have an occasion in another place to take notice. Let us only here consider a little more exactly the fore-mentioned instance of the word *gold*, and we shall see how hard it is precisely to determine its signification. I think all agree, to make it stand for a body of a certain yellow shining colour; which being the idea to which children have annexed that name, the shining yellow part of a peacock's tail, is properly to them gold. Others finding fusibility joined with that yellow colour in certain parcels of matter, make of that combination a complex idea to which they give the name *gold* to denote a sort of substances; and so exclude from being *gold* all such yellow shining bodies, as by fire will be reduced to ashes, and admit to be of that species, or to be comprehended under that name *gold* only such substances as having that shining yellow colour will by fire be reduced to fusion, and not to ashes. Another by the same reason adds the weight, which being a quality, as straightly joined with that colour, as its fusibility, he thinks has the same reason to be joined in its idea, and to be signified by its name: and therefore the other made up of body, of such a colour and fusibility, to be imperfect; and so on of all the rest: wherein no one can show a reason, why some of the inseparable qualities, that are always united in nature, should be put into the nominal essence, and others left out: Or why the word *gold*, signifying that sort of body the ring on his finger is made of, should determine that sort, rather by its colour, weight, and fusibility; than by its colour, weight, and solubility in *aqua regia*: since the dissolving it by that liquor, is as inseparable from it, as the fusion by fire; and they are both of them nothing, but the relation which that substance has to two other bodies, which have a power to operate differently upon it. For by what right is it, that fusibility comes to be a part of the essence, signified by the word *gold*, and solubility but a property of it? Or why is its colour part of the essence, and its malleableness but a property? That which I mean, is this, that these being all but properties, depending on its real constitution; and nothing but powers, either active or passive, in reference to other bodies, no one has authority to determine the signification of the word *gold*, (as referred to such a body existing in nature) more to one collection of ideas to be found in that body, than to another: whereby the signification of that name must unavoidably be very uncertain. Since, as has been said, several people observe several properties in the same substance; and, I think, I may say nobody all. And therefore we have but very imperfect descriptions of things, and words have very uncertain significations.

§18. From what has been said, it is easy to observe, what has been before remarked, *viz.* that the *names of simple ideas are*, of all others the *least liable to mistakes*, and that for these reasons. *First*, Because the ideas they stand for, being each but one single perception, are much easier got, and more clearly retained, than the more complex ones, and therefore are not liable to the uncertainty, which usually attends those compounded ones of *substances and mixed modes*, in which the precise number of simple ideas, that make them up, are not easily agreed, and so readily kept in mind. And *secondly*, because they are never referred to any other essence, but barely that perception they immediately signify: which reference is that, which renders the signification of the names of substances naturally so perplexed, and gives occasion to so many disputes. Men that do not perversely use their words, or on purpose set themselves to cavil, seldom mistake in any language, which they are acquainted with, the use and signification of the names of simple ideas: *white* and *sweet*, *yellow* and *bitter*, carry a very obvious meaning with them, which everyone precisely comprehends, or easily perceives he is ignorant of, and seeks to be informed. But what precise

The names of simple ideas the least doubtful

collection of simple ideas, *modesty*, or *frugality* stand for in another's use, is not so certainly known. And however we are apt to think, we well enough know, what is meant by *gold* or *iron*; yet the precise complex idea, others make them the signs of, is not so certain: and I believe it is very seldom that in speaker and hearer, they stand for exactly the same collection. Which must needs produce mistakes and disputes, when they are made use of in discourses, wherein men have to do with universal propositions, and would settle in their minds universal truths and consider the consequences, that follow from them.

And next to them simple modes §19. By the same rule, the *names of simple modes are next to those of simple ideas, least liable to doubt and uncertainty*, especially those of figure and number, of which men have so clear and distinct ideas. Whoever, that had a mind to understand them, mistook the ordinary meaning of *seven*, or *a triangle*? And in general the least compounded ideas in every kind have the least dubious names.

The most doubtful are the names of very compounded mixed modes and substances §20. Mixed modes therefore, that are made up but of a few and obvious simple ideas, have usually names of no very uncertain signification. But the names of *mixed modes*, which comprehend a great number of simple ideas, are commonly of a very doubtful, and undetermined meaning, as has been shown. The names of substances, being annexed to ideas, that are neither the real essences, nor exact representations of the patterns they are referred to, are liable yet to greater imperfection and uncertainty, especially when we come to a philosophical use of them.

§21. The great disorder that happens *Why this*
in our names of substances, proceeding *imperfection charged*
for the most part from our want of know- *upon words*
ledge, and inability to penetrate into their real constitutions, it may probably be wondered, *why I charge this
as an imperfection*, rather *upon our words* than understandings. This exception, has so much appearance of justice,
that I think myself obliged to give a reason, why I have
followed this method. I must confess then, that when I
first began this discourse of the understanding, and a
good while after, I had not the least thought, that any
consideration of words was at all necessary to it. But
when having passed over the original and composition
of our ideas, I began to examine the extent and certainty
of our knowledge, I found it had so near a connexion with
words, that unless their force and manner of signification
were first well observed, there could be very little said
clearly and pertinently concerning knowledge: which
being conversant about truth, had constantly to do with
propositions. And though it terminated in things, yet it
was for the most part so much by the intervention
of words, that they seemed scarce separable from our
general knowledge. At least they interpose themselves
so much between our understandings, and the truth,
which it would contemplate and apprehend, that like
the *medium* through which visible objects pass, their
obscurity and disorder does not seldom cast a mist before
our eyes, and impose upon our understandings. If we
consider, in the fallacies, men put upon themselves, as
well as others, and the mistakes in men's disputes and
notions, how great a part is owing to words, and their

uncertain or mistaken significations, we shall have reason to think this no small obstacle in the way to knowledge, which, I conclude we are the more carefully to be warned of, because it has been so far from being taken notice of as an inconvenience, that the arts of improving it have been made the business of men's study; and obtained the reputation of learning and subtlety, as we shall see in the following chapter. But I am apt to imagine, that were the imperfections of language, as the instrument of knowledge, more throughly weighed, a great many of the controversies that make such a noise in the world, would of themselves cease; and the way to knowledge, and, perhaps, peace too, lie a great deal opener than it does.

This should teach us moderation, in imposing our own sense of old authors §22. Sure I am, that the signification of words, in all languages, depending very much on the thoughts, notions, and ideas of him that uses them, must unavoidably be of great uncertainty, to men of the same language and country. This is so evident in the Greek authors, that he, that shall peruse their writings, will find, in almost every one of them, a distinct language, though the same words. But when to this natural difficulty in every country, there shall be added different countries, and remote ages, wherein the speakers and writers had very different notions, tempers, customs, ornaments, and figures of speech, *etc.* every one of which, influenced the signification of their words then, though to us now they are lost and unknown, *it would become us to be charitable one to another in our interpretations or misunderstanding of those ancient writings*, which though of great concernment to us to be understood, are liable to the unavoidable difficulties of speech, which, (if we except the names of simple ideas, and some very obvious things) is not capable, without a constant defining the terms of conveying the sense and intention of the speaker, without any manner of doubt and uncertainty, to the hearer. And in discourses of religion, law, and morality, as they are matters of the highest concernment, so there will be the greatest difficulty.

§23. The volumes of interpreters, and commentators on the Old and New Testament, are but too manifest proofs of this. Though everything said in the text be infallibly true, yet the reader may be, nay cannot choose but be very fallible in the understanding of it. Nor is it to be wondered, that the will of GOD, when clothed in words, should be liable to that doubt and uncertainty, which unavoidably attends that sort of conveyance, when even his Son, whilst clothed in flesh, was subject to all the frailties and inconveniencies of human nature, sin excepted. And we ought to magnify his goodness, that he hath spread before all the world, such legible characters of his works and providence, and given all mankind so sufficient a light of reason, that they to whom this written word never came, could not (whenever they set themselves to search) either doubt of the being of a GOD, or of the obedience due to Him. Since then the precepts of natural religion are plain, and very intelligible to all mankind, and seldom come to be controverted; and other revealed truths, which are conveyed to us by books and languages, are liable to the common and natural obscurities and difficulties incident to words, methinks it would become us to be more careful and diligent in observing the former, and less magisterial, positive, and imperious, in imposing our own sense and interpretations of the latter.

Of the Abuse of Words

Abuse of words §1. Besides the imperfection that is naturally in language, and the obscurity and confusion that is so hard to be avoided in the use of words, there are several *wilful faults and neglects*, which men are guilty of, in this way of communication, whereby they render these signs less clear and distinct in their signification, than naturally they need to be.

First, words without §2. *First*, in this kind, the first and most *any, or without* palpable abuse is, the using of words, with-*clear ideas* out clear and distinct ideas; or, which is worse, signs without anything signified. Of these there are two sorts:

I. One may observe, in all languages, certain words, that if they be examined, will be found, in their first original, and their appropriated use, not to stand for any clear and distinct ideas. These, for the most part, the several sects of philosophy and religion have introduced. For their authors, or promoters, either affecting something singular, and out of the way of common apprehensions, or to support some strange opinions, or cover some weakness of their hypothesis, seldom fail to *coin* new words, and such as, when they come to be examined, may justly be called *insignificant terms*. For having either had no determinate collection of ideas annexed to them, when they were first invented; or at least such as, if well examined, will be found inconsistent, 'tis no wonder if afterwards, in the vulgar use of the same party, they remain empty sounds, with little or no signification, amongst those who think it enough to have them often in their mouths, as the distinguishing characters of their church, or school, without much troubling their heads to examine, what are the precise ideas they stand for. I shall not need here to heap up instances, everyone's reading and conversation will sufficiently furnish him: Or if he wants to be better stored, the great mint-masters of these kind of terms, I mean the School-men and metaphysicians, (under which, I think, the disputing natural and moral philosophers of these latter ages, may be comprehended,) have wherewithal abundantly to content him.

§3. II. Others there be, who extend this abuse yet further, who take so little care to lay by words, which in their primary notation have scarce any clear and distinct ideas which they are annexed to, that by an unpardonable negligence, they familiarly *use words*, which the propriety of language has affixed to very important ideas, *without any distinct meaning* at all. *Wisdom*, *glory*, *grace*, etc. are words frequent enough in every man's mouth; but if a great many of those who use them, should be asked, what they mean by them? they would be at a stand, and not know what to answer: a plain proof, that though they have learned those sounds, and have them ready at their tongues' end, yet there are no determined ideas laid up in their minds, which are to be expressed to others by them.

Occasioned by
learning names
before the ideas
they belong to

§4. *Men*, having been *accustomed* from their cradles *to learn words*, which are easily got and retained, *before they knew*, or had framed *the complex ideas*, to which they were annexed, or which were to be found in the things *they* were thought to *stand* for, they *usually continue to do so* all their lives, and without taking the pains necessary to settle in their minds determined ideas, they use their words for such unsteady and confused notions as they have, contenting themselves with the same words other people use; as if their very sound necessarily carried with it constantly the same meaning. This, though men make a shift with, in the ordinary occurrences of life, where they find it necessary to be understood, and therefore they make signs till they are so: yet this insignificancy in their words, when they come to reason concerning either their tenets or interest, manifestly fills their discourse with abundance of empty unintelligible noise and jargon, especially in moral matters, where the words, for the most part, standing for arbitrary and numerous collections of ideas, not regularly and permanently united in nature, their bare sounds are often only thought on, or at least very obscure and uncertain notions annexed to them. Men take the words they find in use amongst their neighbours; and that they may not seem ignorant what they stand for, use them confidently, without much troubling their heads about a certain fixed meaning; whereby, besides the ease of it, they obtain this advantage, that as in such discourses they seldom are in the right, so they are as seldom to be convinced, that they are in the wrong; it being all one to go about to draw those men out of their mistakes, who have no settled notions, as to dispossess a vagrant of his habitation, who has no settled abode. This I guess to be so; and everyone may observe in himself and others, whether it be, or no.

§5. *Secondly*, another great abuse of words is, *inconstancy* in the use of them. It is hard to find a discourse written of any subject, especially of controversy, whereon one shall not observe, if he read with attention, the same words (and those commonly the most material in the discourse, and upon which the argument turns) used sometimes for one collection of simple ideas, and sometimes for another, which is a perfect abuse of language, words being intended for signs of my ideas, to make them known to others, not by any natural signification, but by a voluntary imposition, 'tis plain cheat and abuse, when I make them stand sometimes for one thing, and sometimes for another; the wilful doing whereof, can be imputed to nothing but great folly, or greater dishonesty. And a man, in his accounts with another, may, with as much fairness, make the characters of numbers stand sometimes for one, and sometimes for another collection of units: *v.g.* this character 3 stand sometimes for three, sometimes for four, and sometimes for eight; as in his discourse, or reasoning, make the same words stand for different collections of simple ideas. If men should do so in their reckonings, I wonder who would have to do with them? One who would speak thus, in the affairs and business of the world, and call 8 sometimes seven, and sometimes nine, as best served his advantage, would presently have clapped upon him one of the two names men constantly are disgusted with. And yet in arguings, and learned contests, the same sort of proceeding passes commonly for wit and learning: but to me it appears a greater dishonesty, than the misplacing of counters, in the casting up a debt; and the cheat the greater, by how much truth is of greater concernment and value, than money.

Thirdly, affected obscurity by wrong application §6. *Thirdly*, another abuse of language is, an *affected obscurity*, by either applying old words, to new and unusual significations; or introducing new and ambiguous terms, without defining either; or else putting them so together, as may confound their ordinary meaning. Though the Peripatetic philosophy has been most eminent in this way, yet other sects have not been wholly clear of it. There is scarce any of them that are not cumbered with some difficulties, (such is the imperfection of human knowledge,) which they have been fain to cover with obscurity of terms, and to confound the signification of words, which, like a mist before people's eyes, might hinder their weak parts from being discovered. That *body* and *extension*, in common use, stand for two distinct ideas, is plain to anyone that will but reflect a little. For were their signification precisely the same, it would be proper, and as intelligible to say, the *body of an extension*, as *the extension of a body*; and yet there are those who find it necessary to confound their signification. To this abuse, and the mischiefs of confounding the signification of words, logic, and the liberal sciences as they have been handled in the Schools, have given reputation; and the admired art of disputing, hath added much to the natural imperfection of languages, whilst it has been made use of, and fitted, to perplex the signification of words, more than to discover the knowledge and truth of things: and he that will look into that sort of learned writings, will find the words there much more obscure, uncertain, and undetermined in their meaning, than they are in ordinary conversation.

§7. This is unavoidably to be so, *Logic and dispute* where men's parts and learning, are esti- *has much contributed* mated by their skill in *disputing*. And if *to this* reputation and reward shall attend these conquests, which depend mostly on the fineness and niceties of words, 'tis no wonder if the wit of man so employed, should perplex, involve, and subtilize the signification of sounds, so as never to want something to say, in opposing or defending any question; the victory being adjudged not to him who had truth on his side, but the last word in the dispute.

§8. This, though a very useless skill, and *Calling it subtlety* that which I think the direct opposite to the ways of knowledge, hath yet passed hitherto under the laudable and esteemed names of *subtlety* and *acuteness*; and has had the applause of the Schools, and encouragement of one part of the learned men of the world. And no wonder, since the philosophers of old, (the disputing and wrangling philosophers I mean, such as Lucian wittily, and with reason taxes,) and the Schoolmen since, aiming at glory and esteem, for their great and universal know-ledge, easier a great deal to be pretended to, than really acquired, found this a good expedient to cover their ignorance, with a curious and unexplicable web of per-plexed words, and procure to themselves the admiration of others, by unintelligible terms, the apter to produce wonder, because they could not be understood: whilst it appears in all history, that these profound doctors were no wiser, nor more useful than their neighbours; and brought but small advantage to human life, or the societies, wherein they lived: unless the coining of new words, where they produced no new things to apply them to, or the perplexing or obscuring the signification of old ones, and so bringing all things into question and dispute, were a thing profitable to the life of man, or worthy commendation and reward.

This learning very §9. For, notwithstanding these learned
little benefits society disputants, these all-knowing doctors, it was to the unscholastic statesman, that the governments of the world owed their peace, defence, and liberties; and from the illiterate and contemned mechanic, (a name of disgrace) that they received the improvements of useful arts. Nevertheless, this artificial ignorance, and *learned gibberish*, prevailed mightily in these last ages, by the interest and artifice of those, who found no easier way to that pitch of authority and dominion they have attained, than by amusing the men of business, and ignorant, with hard words, or employing the ingenious and idle in intricate disputes, about unintelligible terms, and holding them perpetually entangled in that endless labyrinth. Besides, there is no such way to gain admittance, or give defence to strange and absurd doctrines, as to guard them round about with legions of obscure, doubtful, and undefined words. Which yet make these retreats, more like the dens of robbers, or holes of foxes, than the fortresses of fair warriors: which if it be hard

to get them out of, it is not for the strength that is in them, but the briars and thorns, and the obscurity of the thickets they are beset with. For untruth being unacceptable to the mind of man, there is no other defence left for absurdity, but obscurity.

§10. Thus learned ignorance, and this art of keeping, even inquisitive men, from true knowledge, hath been propagated in the world, and hath much perplexed, whilst it *But destroys the instruments of knowledge and communication* pretended to inform the understanding. For we see, that other well-meaning and wise men, whose education and parts had not acquired that *acuteness*, could intelligibly express themselves to one another; and in its plain use, make a benefit of language. But though unlearned men well enough understood the words *white* and *black*, *etc.* and had constant notions of the ideas signified by those words; yet there were philosophers found, who had learning and *subtlety* enough to prove, that *snow* was *black*; *i.e.* to prove, that *white* was *black*. Whereby they had the advantage to destroy the instruments and means of discourse, conversation, instruction, and society; whilst with great art and *subtlety* they did no more but perplex and confound the signification of words, and thereby render language less useful, than the real defects of it had made it, a gift, which the illiterate had not attained to.

§11. These learned men did equally instruct men's understandings, and *As useful as to confound the sound of the letters* profit their lives, as he who should alter the signification of known characters, and, by a subtle device of learning, far surpassing the capacity of the illiterate, dull, and vulgar, should, in his writing, show, that he could put *A* for *B*, and *D* for *E*, *etc.* to the no small admiration and benefit of his reader. It being as senseless to put *black*, which is a word agreed on to stand for one sensible idea, to put it, I say, for another, or the contrary idea, *i.e.* to call *snow black*, as to put this mark *A.* which is a character agreed on to stand for one modification of sound, made by a certain motion of the organs of speech, for *B.* which is agreed on to stand for another modification of sound, made by another certain motion of the organs of speech.

This art has perplexed religion and justice §12. Nor hath this mischief stopped in logical niceties, or curious empty speculations; it hath invaded the great concernments of human life and society; obscured and perplexed the material truths of law and divinity; brought confusion, disorder and uncertainty into the affairs of mankind; and if not destroyed, yet in great measure rendered useless, those two great rules, religion and justice. What have the greatest part of the comments and disputes, upon the laws of GOD and man served for, but to make the meaning more doubtful, and perplex the sense? What have been the effect of those multiplied curious distinctions, and acute niceties, but obscurity and uncertainty, leaving the words more unintelligible, and the reader more at a loss? How else comes it to pass, that princes, speaking or writing to their servants, in their ordinary commands, are easily understood; speaking to their people, in their laws, are not so? And, as I remarked before, doth it not often happen, that a man of an ordinary capacity, very well understands a text, or a law, that he reads, till he consults an expositor, or goes to council;

who by that time he hath done explaining them, makes the words signify either nothing at all, or what he pleases.

§13. Whether any by-interests of these professions have occasioned this, *And ought not to pass for learning* I will not here examine; but I leave it to be considered, whether it would not be well for mankind, whose concernment it is to know things as they are, and to do what they ought; and not to spend their lives in talking about them, or tossing words to and fro; whether it would not be well, I say, that the use of words were made plain and direct; and that language, which was given us for the improvement of knowledge, and bond of society, should not be employed to darken truth, and unsettle people's rights; to raise mists, and render unintelligible both morality and religion? Or that at least, if this will happen, it should not be thought learning or knowledge to do so?

§14. *Fourthly,* another great *abuse of words is, the taking them for things.* This, *Fourthly, taking them for things* though it, in some degree, concerns all names in general; yet more particularly affects those of substances. To this abuse, those men are most subject, who confine their thoughts to any one system, and give themselves up into a firm belief of the perfection of any received hypothesis: whereby they come to be persuaded, that the terms of that sect, are so suited to the nature of things, that they perfectly correspond with their real existence. Who is there, that has been bred up in the Peripatetic philosophy, who does not think the ten names, under which are ranked the ten predicaments, to be exactly conformable to the nature of things? Who is there, of that school, that is not persuaded, that *substantial forms, vegetative souls, abhorrence of a vacuum, intentional species,* etc. are something real? These words men have learned from their very entrance upon knowledge, and have found their masters and systems lay great stress upon them: and therefore they cannot quit the opinion, that they are conformable to nature, and are the representations of something that really exists. The Platonists have their *soul of the world,* and the Epicureans their *endeavour towards motion* in their atoms, when at rest. There is scarce any sect in philosophy has not a distinct set of terms, that others understand not. But yet this gibberish, which in the weakness of human understanding, serves so well to palliate men's ignorance, and cover their errors, comes by familiar use amongst those of the same tribe, to seem the most important part of language, and of all other the terms the most significant: and should *aerial* and *ætherial vehicles* come once, by the prevalency of that doctrine, to be generally received anywhere, no doubt those terms would make impressions on men's minds, so as to establish them in the persuasion of the reality of such things, as much as *peripatetic forms,* and *intentional species* have heretofore done.

Instance in matter   §15. How much *names taken for things,* are apt to *mislead the understanding,* the attentive reading of philosophical writers would abundantly discover; and that, perhaps, in words little suspected of any such misuse. I shall instance in one only, and that a very familiar one. How many intricate disputes have there been about *matter,* as if there were some such thing really in nature, distinct from *body;* as 'tis evident, the word *matter* stands for an idea distinct from the idea of body? For if the ideas these two terms stood for, were precisely the same, they might indifferently in all places be put one for another. But we see, that though it be proper to say, there is *one matter of all bodies*, one cannot say, there is *one body of all matters*: we familiarly say, one *body* is bigger than another, but it sounds harsh (and I think is never used) to say, one *matter* is bigger than another. Whence comes this then? *Viz.* from hence, that though *matter* and *body*, be not really distinct, but wherever there is the one, there is the other; yet *matter* and *body*, stand for two different conceptions, whereof the one is incomplete, and but a part of the other. For *body* stands for a solid extended figured substance, whereof *matter* is but a partial and more confused conception, it seeming to me to be used for the substance and solidity of body, without taking in its extension and figure: And therefore it is that speaking of *matter*, we speak of it always as one, because in truth, it expressly contains nothing but the idea of a solid substance, which is everywhere the same, everywhere uniform. This being our idea of *matter*, we no more conceive, or speak of different *matters* in the world, than we do of different solidities; though we both conceive, and speak of different bodies, because extension and figure are capable of variation. But since solidity cannot exist without extension, and figure, the taking *matter* to be the name of something really existing under that precision, has no doubt produced those obscure and unintelligible discourses and disputes, which have filled the heads and books of philosophers concerning *materia prima*; which imperfection or abuse, how far it may concern a great many other general terms, I leave to be con sidered. This, I think, I may at least say, that we should have a great many fewer disputes in the world, if words were taken for what they are, the signs of our ideas only, and not for things themselves. For when we argue about *matter*, or any the like term, we truly argue only about the idea we express by that sound, whether that precise idea agree to anything really existing in nature, or no. And if men would tell, what ideas they make their words stand for, there could not be half that obscurity or wrangling, in the search or support of truth, that there is.

This makes errors lasting   §16. But whatever inconvenience follows from this mistake of words, this I am sure, that by constant and familiar use, they charm men into notions far remote from the truth of things. 'Twould be a hard matter, to persuade anyone, that the words which his father or schoolmaster, the parson of the parish, or such a reverend doctor used, signified nothing that really existed in nature: which, perhaps, is *none of the least causes, that men are so hardly drawn to quit their mistakes,* even in opinions purely philosophical, and where they have no other interest but truth. For the words, they have a long time been used to, remaining firm in their minds, 'tis no wonder, that the wrong notions annexed to them, should not be removed.

Fifthly, setting them for what they cannot signify   §17. *Fifthly,* another *abuse of words, is the setting them in the place of things, which they do or can by no means signify.* We may observe, that in the general names of substances, whereof the nominal essences are only known to us, when we put them into propositions, and affirm or deny anything about them, we do most commonly tacitly suppose, or intend, they should stand for the real essence of a certain sort of substances. For when a man says 'gold is malleable', he means and would insinuate something more than this, that 'what I call gold is malleable', (though truly it amounts to no more) but would have this understood, *viz*. that 'gold; i.e. what has the real essence of gold is malleable', which amounts to thus much, that 'malleableness depends on, and is inseparable from the real essence of gold'. But a man, not knowing wherein that real essence consists, the connexion in his mind of malleableness, is not truly with an essence he knows not, but only with the sound gold he puts for it. Thus when we say, that *animal rational* is, and *animal implume bipes latis unguibus*, ['featherless broad-nailed biped'. A traditional definition stemming from Plato] is not a good definition of a man; 'tis plain, we suppose the name *man* in this case to stand for the real essence of a species, and would signify, that a *rational animal* better described that real essence, than *a two-legged animal with broad nails, and without feathers*. For else, why might not Plato as properly make the word ἄνθρωπος or *man* stand for his complex idea, made up of the ideas of a body, distinguished from others by a certain shape and other outward appearances, as Aristotle, make the complex idea, to which he gave the name ἄνθρωπος or *man*, of body, and the faculty of reasoning joined together; unless the name ἄνθρωπος or *man*, were supposed to stand for something else, than what it signifies; and to be put in the place of some other thing, than the idea a man professes he would express by it?

John Locke

V.g. putting them for
the real essences of
substances

§18. 'Tis true, the names of substances would be much more useful, and propositions made in them much more certain, were the real essences of substances the ideas in our minds, which those words signified. And 'tis for want of those real essences, that our words convey so little knowledge or certainty in our discourses about them: and therefore the mind, to remove that imperfection as much as it can, makes them, by a secret supposition, to stand for a thing, having that real essence, as if thereby it made some nearer approaches to it. For though the word *man* or *gold*, signify nothing truly but a complex idea of properties, united together in one sort of substances: yet there is scarce anybody in the use of these words, but often supposes each of those names to stand for a thing having the real essence, on which those properties depend. Which is so far from diminishing the imperfection of our words, that by a plain abuse, it adds to it, when we would make them stand for something, which not being in our complex idea, the name we use, can no ways be the sign of.

Hence we think every
change of our idea in
substances, not to
change the species

§19. This shows us the reason, Why in *mixed modes* any of the ideas that make the composition of the complex one, being left out, or changed, it is allowed to be another thing, *i.e.* to be of another species, as is plain in *chance-medly, manslaughter, murder, parricide*, etc. The reason whereof is, because the complex idea signified by that name, is the real, as well as nominal essence; and there is no secret reference of that name to any other essence, but that. But in *substances* it is not so. For though

100

in that called *gold* one puts into his complex idea, what another leaves out; and *vice versâ*: yet men do not usually think, that therefore the species is changed: because they secretly in their minds refer that name, and suppose it annexed to a real immutable essence of a thing existing, on which those properties depend. He that adds to his complex idea of *gold*, that of fixedness or solubility in *aqua regia*, which he put not in it before, is not thought to have changed the species; but only to have a more perfect idea, by adding another simple idea, which is always in fact, joined with those other, of which his former complex idea consisted. But this reference of the name to a thing, whereof we have not the idea, is so far from helping at all, that it only serves the more to involve us in difficulties. For by this tacit reference to the real essence of that species of bodies, the word *gold* (which by standing for a more or less perfect collection of simple ideas, serves to design that sort of body well enough in civil discourse) comes to have no signification at all, being put for somewhat, whereof we have no idea at all, and so can signify nothing at all, when the body itself is away. For however it may be thought all one; yet, if well considered, it will be found a quite different thing, to argue about *gold* in name, and about a parcel of the body itself, *v.g.* a piece of *leaf-gold* laid before us; though in discourse we are fain to substitute the name for the thing.

§20. That which, I think very much disposes men to substitute their names for the real essences of species, is the supposition before mentioned, that nature

The cause of the abuse, a supposition of nature's working always regularly

works regularly in the production of things, and sets the boundaries to each of those species, by giving exactly the same real internal constitution to each individual, which we rank under one general name. Whereas anyone who observes their different qualities can hardly doubt, that many of the individuals, called by the same name, are, in their internal constitution, as different one from another, as several of those which are ranked under different specific names. *This supposition*, however *that the same precise internal constitution goes always with the same specific name, makes men forward to take* those *names for the representatives* of those real *essences*, though indeed they signify nothing but the complex ideas they have in their minds, when they use them. So that, if I may so say, signifying one thing, and being supposed for, or put in the place of another, they cannot but, in such a kind of use, cause a great deal of uncertainty in men's discourses; especially in those, who have thoroughly imbibed the doctrine of *substantial forms*, whereby they firmly imagine the several species of things to be determined and distinguished.

This abuse contains §21. But however preposterous and *two false suppositions* absurd it be, to make our names stand for ideas we have not, or (which is all one) essences that we know not, it being in effect to make our words the signs of nothing; yet 'tis evident to anyone, whoever so little reflects on the use men make of their words, that there is nothing more familiar. When a man asks, whether this or that thing he sees, let it be a drill, or a monstrous *fœtus*, be a *man*, or no; 'tis evident, the question is not, whether that particular thing agree to his complex idea, expressed by the name *man*: but whether it has in it the real essence of a species of things, which he supposes his name *man* to stand for. In which way of using the names of substances, there are these false suppositions contained.

First, that there are certain precise essences, according to which nature makes all particular things, and by which they are distinguished into species. That every thing has a real constitution, whereby it is what it is, and on which its sensible qualities depend, is past doubt: But I think it has been proved, that this makes not the distinction of species, as we rank them; nor the boundaries of their names.

Secondly, this tacitly also insinuates, as if we had ideas of these proposed essences. For to what purpose else is it, to inquire whether this or that thing have the real essence of the species *man*, if we did not suppose that there were such a specific essence known? Which yet is utterly false: and therefore such application of names, as would make them stand for ideas which we have not, must needs cause great disorder in discourses and reasonings about them, and be a great inconvenience in our communication by words.

§22. *Sixthly*, there remains yet another more general, though, perhaps, less observed *abuse of words*; and that is, that men having by a long and familiar use annexed to them certain ideas, they are apt *to imagine so near and necessary a connexion between the names and the signification* they use them in, that they forwardly suppose one cannot but understand what their meaning is; and

Sixthly, a supposition that words have a certain and evident signification

therefore one ought to acquiesce in the words delivered, as if it were past doubt, that in the use of those common received sounds, the speaker and hearer had necessarily the same precise ideas. Whence presuming, that when they have in discourse used any term, they have thereby, as it were, set before others the very thing they talk of. And so likewise taking the words of others, as naturally standing for just what they themselves have been accustomed to apply them to, they never trouble themselves to explain their own, or understand clearly others' meaning. From whence commonly proceeds noise, and wrangling, without improvement of information; whilst men take words to be the constant regular marks of agreed notions, which in truth are no more but the voluntary and unsteady signs of their own ideas. And yet men think it strange, if in discourse, or (where it is often absolutely necessary) in dispute, one sometimes asks the meaning of their terms: though the arguings one may every day observe in conversation, make it evident, that there are few names of complex ideas, which any two men use for the same just precise collection. 'Tis hard to name a word, which will not be a clear instance of this. *Life* is a term, none more familiar. Anyone almost would take it for an affront, to be asked what he meant by it. And yet if it comes in question, whether a plant, that lies ready formed in the seed, have life; whether the embryo in an egg before incubation, or a man in a swoon without sense or motion, be alive, or no? it is easy to perceive, that a clear distinct settled idea does not always accompany the use of so known a word, as that of *life* is. Some gross and confused conceptions men indeed ordinarily have, to which they apply the common words of their language, and such a loose use of their words serves them well enough in their ordinary discourses or affairs. But this is not sufficient for philosophical inquiries. Knowledge and reasoning require precise determinate ideas. And though men will not be so importunately dull, as not to understand what others say, without demanding an explication of their terms; nor so troublesomely critical, as to correct others in the use of the words they receive from them: yet where truth and knowledge are concerned in the case, I know not what fault it can be to desire the explication of words, whose sense seems dubious; or why a man should be ashamed to own his ignorance, in what sense another man uses his words, since he has no other way of certainly knowing it, but by being informed. This abuse of taking words upon trust, has nowhere spread so far, nor with so ill effects, as amongst men of letters. The multiplication and obstinacy of disputes, which has so laid waste the intellectual world, is owing to nothing more, than to this ill use of words. For though it be generally believed, that there is great diversity of opinions in the volumes and variety of controversies, the world is distracted with; yet the most I can find, that the contending learned men of different parties do, in their arguings one with another, is, that they speak different languages. For I am apt to imagine, that when any of them quitting terms, think upon things, and know what they think, they think all the same: though perhaps, what they would have, be different.

§23. To conclude this consideration of the imperfection, and abuse of language; the *ends of language in our discourse with others*, being chiefly these three: *first, to make known* one man's thoughts or ideas to another. *Secondly*, to do it *with* as much ease and *quickness*, as is possible; and *thirdly*, thereby *to convey* the *knowledge* of things. Language is either abused, or deficient, when it fails of any of these three.

The ends of language, first, to convey our ideas

First, words fail in the first of these ends, and lay not open one man's ideas to another's view. *First*, when men have names in their mouths without any determined ideas in their minds, whereof they are the signs: or *secondly*, when they apply the common received names of any language to ideas, to which the common use of that language does not apply them: or *thirdly*, when they apply them very unsteadily, making them stand now for one, and by and by for another idea.

§24. *Secondly*, men fail of conveying their thoughts, with all the quickness and ease that may be, when they have complex ideas, without having distinct names for them. This is sometimes the fault of the language itself, which has not in it a sound yet applied to such a signification: and sometimes the fault of the man, who has not yet learned the name for that idea he would show another.

Secondly, to do it with quickness

§25. *Thirdly*, there is no knowledge of things conveyed by men's words, when their ideas agree not to the reality of things. Though it be a defect, that has its original in our ideas, which are not so conformable to the nature of

Thirdly, therewith to convey the knowledge of things

things, as attention, study, and application might make them: yet it fails not to extend itself to our words too, when we use them as signs of real beings, which yet never had any reality or existence.

§26. *First*, he that hath words of any language, without distinct ideas in his mind, to which he applies them, does, so far as he uses them in discourse, only make a noise without any sense or signification; and how learned soever he may seem by the use of hard words, or learned terms, is not much more advanced thereby in knowledge, than he would be in learning, who had nothing in his study but the bare titles of books, without possessing the contents of them. For all such words, however put into discourse, according to the right construction of grammatical rules, or the harmony of well-turned periods, do yet amount to nothing but bare sounds, and nothing else.

How men's words fail in all these

§27. *Secondly*, he that has complex ideas, without particular names for them, would be in no better a case than a bookseller, who had in his warehouse volumes, that lay there unbound, and without titles; which he could therefore make known to others, only by showing the loose sheets, and communicate them only by tale. This man is hindered in his discourse, for want of words to communicate his complex ideas, which he is therefore forced to make known by an enumeration of the simple ones that compose them; and so is fain often to use twenty words, to express what another man signifies in one.

§28. *Thirdly*, he that puts not constantly the same sign for the same idea, but uses the same words sometimes in one, and sometimes in another signification, ought to pass in the Schools and conversation, for as fair a man, as he does in the market and exchange, who sells several things under the same name.

§29. *Fourthly*, he that applies the words of any language to ideas, different from those, to which the common use of that country applies them, however his own understanding may be filled with truth and light, will not by such words be able to convey much of it to others, without defining his terms. For however, the sounds are such as are familiarly known, and easily enter the ears of those who are accustomed to them; yet standing for other ideas than those they usually are annexed to, and are wont to excite in the mind of the hearers, they cannot make known the thoughts of him who thus uses them.

§30. *Fifthly*, he that hath imagined to himself substances such as never have been, and filled his head with ideas which have not any correspondence with the real nature of things, to which yet he gives settled and defined names, may fill his discourse, and perhaps, another man's head, with the fantastical imaginations of his own brain; but will be very far from advancing thereby one jot in real and true knowledge.

§31. He that hath names without ideas, wants meaning in his words, and speaks only empty sounds. He that hath complex ideas without names for them, wants liberty and dispatch in his expressions, and is necessitated to use periphrases. He that uses his words loosely and unsteadily, will either be not minded, or not understood. He that applies his names to ideas, different from their common use, wants propriety in his language, and speaks gibberish. And he that hath ideas of substances, disagreeing with the real existence of things, so far wants the materials of true knowledge in his understanding, and hath, instead thereof, chimeras.

§32. In our notions concerning sub- *How in substances* stances we are liable to all the former inconveniencies: *v.g.* 1. He that uses the word *tarantula*, without having any imagination or idea of what it stands for, pronounces a good word; but so long means nothing at all by it. 2. He that, in a new-discovered country, shall see several sorts of animals and vegetables, unknown to him before, may have as true ideas of them, as of a horse, or a stag; but can speak of them only by a description, till he shall either take the names the natives call them by, or give them names himself. 3. He that uses the word *body* sometimes for pure extension, and sometimes for extension and solidity together, will talk very fallaciously. 4. He that gives the name *horse*, to that idea which common usage calls *mule*, talks improperly, and will not be understood. 5. He that thinks the name *centaur* stands for some real being, imposes on himself, and mistakes words for things.

§33. In modes and relations generally, we *How in modes* are liable only to the four first of these incon- *and relations* veniencies, (*viz.*) 1. I may have in my memory the names of modes, as *gratitude*, or *charity*, and yet not have any precise ideas annexed in my thoughts to those names. 2. I may have ideas, and not know the names that belong to them; *v.g.* I may have the idea of a man's drinking, till his colour and humour be altered, till his tongue trips, and his eyes look red, and his feet fail him; and yet not know, that it is to be called *drunkenness*. 3. I may have the ideas of virtues or vices, and names also, but apply them amiss: *v.g.* when I apply the name *frugality* to that idea which others call and signify by this sound, *covetousness*. 4. I may use any of those names with inconstancy. 5. But in modes and relations, I cannot have ideas disagreeing to the existence of things: for modes being complex ideas, made by the mind at pleasure; and relation being but my way of considering, or comparing two things together, and so also an idea of my own making, these ideas can scarce be found to disagree with any thing existing; since they are not in the mind, as the copies of things regularly made by nature, nor as properties inseparably flowing from the internal constitution or essence of any substance; but, as it were, patterns lodged in my memory, with names annexed to them, to denominate actions and relations by, as they come to exist. But the mistake is commonly in my giving a wrong name to my conceptions; and so using words in a different sense from other people, I am not understood, but am thought to have wrong ideas of them, when I give wrong names to them. Only if I put in my ideas of mixed modes or relations, any inconsistent ideas together, I fill my head also with chimeras; since such ideas, if well examined, cannot so much as exist in the mind, much less any real being, be ever denominated from them.

Seventhly, figurative speech also an abuse of language

§34. Since wit and fancy finds easier entertainment in the world, than dry truth and real knowledge, *figurative speeches*, and allusion in language, will hardly be admitted, as *an* imperfection or *abuse* of it. I confess, in discourses, where we seek rather pleasure and delight, than information and improvement, such ornaments as are borrowed from them, can scarce pass for faults. But yet, if we would speak of things as they are, we must allow, that all the art of rhetoric, besides order and clearness, all the artificial and figurative application of words eloquence hath invented, are for nothing else but to insinuate wrong ideas, move the passions, and thereby mislead the judgment; and so indeed are perfect cheat: and therefore however laudable or allowable oratory may render them in harangues and popular addresses, they are certainly, in all discourses that pretend to inform or instruct, wholly to be avoided; and where truth and knowledge are concerned, cannot but be thought a great fault, either of the language or person that makes use of them. What, and how various they are, will be superfluous here to take notice; the books of rhetoric which abound in the world, will instruct those, who want to be informed: only I cannot but observe, how little the preservation and improvement of truth and knowledge, is the care and concern of mankind; since the arts of fallacy are endowed and preferred. 'Tis evident how much men love to deceive, and be deceived, since rhetoric, that powerful instrument of error and deceit, has its established professors, is publicly taught, and has always been had in great reputation: and, I doubt not, but it will be thought great boldness, if not brutality in me to have said thus much against it. *Eloquence*, like the fair sex, has too prevailing beauties in it, to suffer itself ever to be spoken against. And 'tis in vain to find fault with those arts of deceiving, wherein men find pleasure to be deceived.

Of the Remedies of the foregoing Imperfections and Abuses

They are worth seeking §1. The natural and improved imperfections of language, we have seen above at large: and speech being the great bond that holds society together, and the common conduit, whereby the improvements of knowledge are conveyed from one man, and one generation to another, it would well deserve our most serious thoughts, to consider what *remedies* are to be found *for these inconveniences* above-mentioned.

Are not easy §2. I am not so vain to think, that anyone can pretend to attempt the perfect *reforming* the *languages* of the world, no not so much as that of his own country, without rendering himself ridiculous. To require that men should use their words constantly in the same sense, and for none but determined and uniform ideas, would be to think, that all men should have the same notions, and should talk of nothing but what they have clear and distinct ideas of. Which is not to be expected by anyone, who hath not vanity enough to imagine he can prevail with men to be very knowing or very silent. And he must be very little skilled in the world, who thinks that a voluble tongue, shall accompany only a good understanding; or that men's talking much or little, shall hold proportion only to their knowledge.

§3. But though the market and exchange   *But yet necessary* must be left to their own ways of talking,   *to philosophy* and gossipings not be robbed of their ancient privilege: though the Schools, and men of argument would perhaps take it amiss to have anything offered, to abate the length, or lessen the number of their disputes; yet, methinks those, *who* pretend *seriously* to *search after*, or maintain *truth*, should think themselves obliged to study, how they might deliver themselves without obscurity, doubt-fulness, or equivocation, to which men's words are natur-ally liable, if care be not taken.

§4. For he that shall well consider the   *Misuse of words the* *errors* and obscurity, the mistakes and con-   *cause of great errors* fusion, that is *spread in the world by an ill use of words*, will find some reason to doubt, whether language, as it has been employed, has contributed more to the improvement or hindrance of knowledge amongst man-kind. How many are there, that when they would think on things, fix their thoughts only on words, especially when they would apply their minds to moral matters? And who then can wonder, if the result of such contem-plations and reasonings, about little more than sounds, whilst the ideas they annexed to them, are very confused, or very unsteady, or perhaps none at all; who can wonder, I say, that such thoughts and reasonings, end in nothing but obscurity and mistake, without any clear judgement or knowledge?

§5. This inconvenience, in an ill use of words,   *Obstinacy* men suffer in their own private meditations: but much more manifest are the disorders which follow from it, in conversation, discourse, and arguings with others. For language being the great conduit, whereby men convey their discoveries, reasonings, and knowledge, from one to another, he that makes an ill use of it, though he does not corrupt the fountains of knowledge, which are in things themselves; yet he does, as much as in him lies, break or stop the pipes, whereby it is distributed to the public use and advantage of mankind. He that uses words without any clear and steady meaning, what does he but lead himself and others into errors? And he that designedly does it, ought to be looked on as an enemy to truth and knowledge. And yet, who can wonder, that all the sciences and parts of knowledge, have been so over-charged with obscure and equivocal terms, and insignificant and doubtful expressions, capable to make the most attentive or quick-sighted, very little, or not at all the more knowing or orthodox; since subtlety, in those who make profession to teach or defend truth, hath passed so much for a virtue: a virtue, indeed, which consisting, for the most part, in nothing but the fallacious and illusory use of *obscure* or *deceitful terms*, is only fit to *make men* more *conceited* in their ignorance, and *obstinate* in their errors.

And wrangling §6. Let us look into the books of controversy of any kind, there we shall see, that the effect of obscure, unsteady, or equivocal terms, is nothing but noise and wrangling about sounds, without convincing or bettering a man's understanding. For if the idea be not agreed on, betwixt the speaker and hearer, for which the words stand, the argument is not about things, but names. As often as such a word, whose signification is not ascertained betwixt them, comes in use, their understandings have no other object wherein they agree, but barely the sound, the things, that they think on at that time as expressed by that word, being quite different.

§7. Whether a *bat* be a *bird*, or no, is   *Instance bat and bird* not a question, whether a bat be another thing than indeed it is, or have other qualities than indeed it has, for that would be extremely absurd to doubt of: but the question is, 1. either between those that acknowledged themselves to have but imperfect ideas of one or both of those sorts of things, for which these names are supposed to stand; and then it is a real inquiry, concerning the nature of a *bird*, or a *bat*, to make their yet imperfect ideas of it more complete, by examining, whether all the simple ideas, to which combined together, they both give the name *bird*, be all to be found in a *bat*: but this is a question only of inquirers, (not disputers,) who neither affirm, nor deny, but examine: or, 2. it is a question between disputants; whereof the one affirms, and the other denies, that a *bat* is a *bird*. And then the question is barely about the signification of one, or both these words; in that they not having both the same complex ideas, to which they give these two names, one holds, and t'other denies, that these two names may be affirmed one of another. Were they agreed in the signification of these two names, it were impossible they should dispute about them. For they would presently and clearly see, (were that adjusted between them,) whether all the simple ideas, of the more general name *bird*, were found in the complex idea of a *bat*, or no; and so there could be no doubt, whether a *bat* were a *bird*, or no. And here I desire it may be considered, and carefully examined, whether the greatest part of the disputes in the world, are not merely verbal, and about the signification of words; and whether if the terms they are made in, were defined, and reduced in their signification (as they must be where they signify anything) to determined collections of the simple ideas they do or should stand for, those disputes would not end of themselves, and immediately vanish. I leave it then to be considered, what the learning of disputation is, and how well they are employed for the advantage of themselves, or others, whose business is only the vain ostentation of sounds; *i.e.* those who spend their lives in disputes and controversies. When I shall see any of those combatants, strip all his terms of ambiguity and obscurity, (which everyone may do in the words he uses himself) I shall think him a champion for knowledge, truth, and peace, and not the slave of vain-glory, ambition, or a party.

First, remedy to use no word without an idea §8. *To remedy the defects of speech* beforementioned, to some degree, and to prevent the inconveniences that follow from them, I imagine, the observation of these following rules may be of use, till somebody better able shall judge it worth his while, to think more maturely on this matter, and oblige the world with his thoughts on it.

First, a man should take care *to use no word without a signification*, no name without an idea for which he makes it stand. This rule will not seem altogether needless, to anyone who shall take the pains to recollect how often he has met with such words; as *instinct*, *sympathy*, and *antipathy*, etc. in the discourse of others, so made use of, as he might easily conclude, that those that used them, had no ideas in their minds to which they applied them; but spoke them only as sounds, which usually served instead of reasons, on the like occasions. Not but that these words, and the like, have very proper significations in which they may be used; but there being no natural connexion between any words, and any ideas, these, and any other, may be learned by rote, and pronounced or writ by men, who have no ideas in their minds, to which they have annexed them, and for which they make them stand; which is necessary they should, if men would speak intelligibly even to themselves alone.

§9. *Secondly*, 'tis not enough a man *Secondly, to have* uses his *words as signs of* some *ideas*, those *distinct ideas annexed* ideas he annexes them to, if they be *to them in modes* simple, must be clear and distinct; if *complex*, must be *determinate, i.e.* the precise collection of simple ideas settled in the mind, with that sound annexed to it, as the sign of that precise determined collection, and no other. This is very necessary in names of modes, and especially moral words; which having no settled objects in nature, from whence their ideas are taken, as from their original, are apt to be very confused. *Justice* is a word in every man's mouth, but most commonly with a very undetermined loose signification: which will always be so, unless a man has in his mind a distinct comprehension of the component parts, that complex idea consists of; and if it be decompounded, must be able to resolve it still on, till he at last comes to the simple ideas, that make it up: and unless this be done, a man makes an ill use of the word, let it be *justice*, for

example, or any other. I do not say, a man needs stand
to recollect, and make this analysis at large, every time
the word *justice* comes in his way: but this, at least, is
necessary, that he have so examined the signification of
that name, and settled the idea of all its parts in his mind,
that he can do it when he pleases. If one, who makes
his complex idea of *justice*, to be such a treatment of the
person or goods of another, as is according to law, hath
not a clear and distinct idea what *law* is, which makes a
part of his complex idea of justice, 'tis plain, his idea
of justice itself, will be confused and imperfect. This
exactness will, perhaps, be judged very troublesome: and
therefore most men will think, they may be excused
from settling the complex ideas of mixed modes so
precisely in their minds. But yet I must say, till this be
done, it must not be wondered, that they have a great
deal of obscurity and confusion in their own minds, and
a great deal of wrangling in their discourses with others.

And conformable in   §10. In the names of *substances*, for a
substances   right use of them, something more is required than barely *determined* ideas: in these *the names
must also be conformable to things*, as they exist: but of this,
I shall have occasion to speak more at large by and by.
This exactness is absolutely necessary in inquiries after
philosophical knowledge, and in controversies about
truth. And though it would be well too, if it extended
itself to common conversation, and the ordinary affairs
of life; yet I think that is scarce to be expected. Vulgar
notions suit vulgar discourses: and both, though confused
enough, yet serve pretty well the market, and the wake.
Merchants and lovers, cooks and tailors, have words

wherewithal to dispatch their ordinary affairs; and so, I think, might philosophers and disputants too, if they had a mind to understand, and to be clearly understood.

§11. *Thirdly*, 'tis not enough that men   *Thirdly, propriety* have ideas, determined ideas, for which they make these signs stand; but they *must* also take care to *apply their words*, as near as may be, *to such ideas as common use has annexed them to*. For words, especially of languages already framed, being no man's private possession, but the common measure of commerce and communication, 'tis not for anyone, at pleasure, to change the stamp they are current in; nor alter the ideas they are affixed to; or at least when there is a necessity to do so, he is bound to give notice of it. Men's intentions in speaking are, or at least should be, to be understood; which cannot be without frequent explanations, demands, and other the like incommodious interruptions, where men do not follow common use. Propriety of speech, is that which gives our thoughts entrance into other men's minds with the greatest ease and advantage: and therefore deserves some part of our care and study, especially in the names of moral words. The proper signification and use of terms is best to be learned from those, who in their writings and discourses, appear to have had the clearest notions, and applied to them their terms with the exactest choice and fitness. This way of using a man's words, according to the propriety of the language, though it have not always the good fortune to be understood: yet most commonly leaves the blame of it on him, who is so unskilful in the language he speaks, as not to understand it, when made use of, as it ought to be.

Fourthly, to make known their meaning

§12. *Fourthly.* But because common use has not so visibly annexed any signification to words, as to make men know always certainly what they precisely stand for: and because men in the improvement of their knowledge, come to have ideas different from the vulgar and ordinary received ones, for which they must either make new words, (which men seldom venture to do, for fear of being thought guilty of affectation or novelty,) or else must use old ones, in a new signification. Therefore after the observation of the foregoing rules, it is sometimes necessary for the ascertaining the signification of words, to *declare their meaning*; where either common use has left it uncertain and loose; (as it has in most names of very complex ideas) or where the term, being very material in the discourse, and that upon which it chiefly turns, is liable to any doubtfulness or mistake.

And that three ways

§13. As the ideas, men's words stand for, are of different sorts: so the way of making known the ideas, they stand for, when there is occasion, is also different. For though defining be thought the proper *way, to make known the proper signification of words*; yet there be some words, that will not be defined, as there be others, whose precise meaning cannot be made known, but by definition: and, perhaps, a third, which partake somewhat of both the other, as we shall see in the names of simple ideas, modes, and substances.

First, in simple ideas by synonymous terms or showing

§14. *First*, when a man makes use of the *name* of *any simple idea*, which he perceives is not understood, or is in danger to be mistaken, he is obliged by the laws of ingenuity, and the end of speech, to declare his meaning, and make known what idea he makes it stand for. This, as has been shown, cannot be done by definition: and therefore, when a synonymous word fails to do it, there is but one of these ways left. *First*, sometimes the *naming the subject, wherein that simple idea is* to be found, will make its name be understood by those, who are acquainted with that subject, and know it by that name. So to make a countryman understand what *feuillemorte* [yellowish brown] colour signifies, it may suffice to tell him, 'tis the colour of withered leaves falling in autumn. *Secondly*, but the only sure way of making known the signification of the name of any simple idea, is *by presenting to his senses that subject, which may produce it in his mind*, and make him actually have the idea, that word stands for.

§15. *Secondly, mixed modes*, especially those belonging to morality, being most of them such combinations of ideas, as the mind puts together of its own choice; and whereof there are not always standing patterns to be found existing, the signification of their names cannot be made known, as those of simple ideas, by any showing: but in recompense thereof, may be perfectly and exactly *defined*. For they being combinations of several ideas, that the mind of man has arbitrarily put together, without reference to any archetypes, men may, if they please, exactly know the ideas, that go to each compositions, and so both use these words in a certain and undoubted signification, and perfectly declare, when there is occasion, what they stand for. This, if well considered, would lay great blame

Secondly, in mixed modes by definition

on those, who make not their discourses about moral things very clear and distinct. For since the precise signification of the names of mixed modes, or which is all one, the real essence of each species, is to be known, they being not of nature's, but man's making, it is a great negligence and perverseness, to discourse of moral things with uncertainty and obscurity, which is more pardonable in treating of natural substances, where doubtful terms are hardly to be avoided, for a quite contrary reason, as we shall see by and by.

Morality capable of
demonstration
§16. Upon this ground it is, that I am bold to think, that *morality is capable of demonstration*, as well as mathematics: since the precise real essence of the things moral words stand for, may be perfectly known; and so the congruity, or incongruity of the things themselves, be certainly discovered, in which consists perfect knowledge. Nor let anyone object, that the names of substances are often to be made use of in morality, as well as those of modes, from which will arise obscurity. For as to substances, when concerned in moral discourses, their divers natures are not so much inquired into, as supposed; *v.g.* when we say that 'man is subject to law': we mean nothing by *man*, but a corporeal rational creature: what the real essence or other qualities of that creature are in this case, is no way considered. And therefore, whether a child or changeling be a *man* in a physical sense, may amongst the naturalists be as disputable as it will, it concerns not at all the *moral man*, as I may call him, which is this immoveable unchangeable idea, *a corporeal rational being*. For were there a monkey, or any other creature to be found, that

had the use of reason, to such a degree, as to be able to understand general signs, and to deduce consequences about general ideas, he would no doubt be subject to law, and, in that sense, be a *man*, how much soever he differed in shape from others of that name. The names of substances, if they be used in them, as they should, can no more disturb moral, than they do mathematical discourses: where, if the mathematicians speak of a *cube* or *globe* of *gold*, or any other body, he has his clear settled idea, which varies not, though it may, by mistake be applied to a particular body, to which it belongs not.

§17. This I have here mentioned by the by, to show of what consequence it *Definitions can make moral discourses clear* is for men, in their names of mixed modes, and consequently, in all their moral discourses, to define their words when there is occasion: since thereby moral knowledge may be brought, to so great clearness and certainty. And it must be great want of ingenuity, (to say no worse of it) to refuse to do it: since a *definition is the only way, whereby the precise meaning of moral words can be known*; and yet a way, whereby their meaning may be known *certainly*, and without leaving any room for any contest about it. And therefore the negligence or perverseness of mankind, cannot be excused, if their discourses in morality be not much more clear, than those in natural philosophy: since they are about ideas in the mind, which are none of them false or disproportionate; they having no external beings for archetypes which they are referred to, and must correspond with. It is far easier for men to frame in their minds an idea, which shall be the standard to which they will give the name *justice*, with which pattern so made, all actions that agree shall pass under that denomination, than, having seen Aristides, to frame an idea, that shall, in all things, be exactly like him, who is as he is, let men make what idea, they please of him. For the one, they need but know the combination of ideas, that are put together within in their own minds; for the other, they must inquire into the whole nature, and abstruse hidden constitution, and various qualities of a thing existing without them.

And is the only way §18. Another reason that makes the *defining of mixed modes* so necessary, *especially of moral words*, is what I mentioned a little before, *viz.* that it is *the only way whereby the signification of the most of* them can be known with certainty. For the ideas they stand for, being for the most part such, whose component parts nowhere exist together, but scattered and mingled with others, it is the mind alone that collects them, and gives them the union of one idea: and it is only by words, enumerating the several simple ideas which the mind has united, that we can make known to others, what their names stand for; the assistance of the senses in this case not helping us, by the proposal of sensible objects, to show the ideas, which our names of this kind stand for, as it does often in the names of sensible simple ideas, and also to some degree in those of substances.

Thirdly, in substances, §19. *Thirdly, for the explaining* the sig-
by showing and defining nification of *the names of substances* as they stand for the ideas we have of their distinct species, both the forementioned ways, *viz.* of *showing and defining, are requisite*, in many cases, to be made use of. For there being ordinarily in each sort some leading qualities, to

which we suppose the other ideas, which make up our complex idea of that species, annexed, we forwardly give the specific name to that thing, wherein that characteristical mark is found, which we take to be the most distinguishing idea of that species. These leading or characteristical (as I may so call them) ideas, in the sorts of animals and vegetables, is mostly figure, and in inanimate bodies colour, and in some both together. Now,

§20. These *leading sensible qualities* are those, which make *the chief ingredients of our specific ideas*, and consequently the most observable and unvariable part in the definitions of our specific names, as attributed to sorts *of substances* coming under our knowledge. For though the sound *man*, in its own nature, be as apt to signify a complex idea made up of animality and rationality, united in the same subject, as to signify any other combination; yet used as a mark to stand for a sort of creatures we count of our own kind, perhaps the outward shape is as necessary to be taken into our complex idea, signified by the word *man*, as any other we find in it; and therefore why Plato's *animal implume bipes latis unguibus*, [featherless broad-nailed biped] should not be as good a definition of the name *man*, standing for that sort of creatures, will not be easy to show: for 'tis the shape, as the leading quality, that seems more to determine that species, than a faculty of reasoning, which appears not at first, and in some never. And if this be not allowed to be so, I do not know how they can be excused from murder, who kill monstrous births, (as we call them,) because of an

Ideas of the leading qualities of substances, are best got by showing

unordinary shape, without knowing whether they have a rational soul, or no; which can be no more discerned in a well-formed, than ill-shaped infant, as soon as born. And who is it has informed us, that a rational soul can inhabit no tenement, unless it has just such a sort of frontispiece, or can join itself to, and inform no sort of body, but one that is just of such an outward structure.

§21. Now *these leading qualities, are best made known by showing* and can hardly be made known otherwise. For the shape of an *horse*, or *cassowary*, will be but rudely and imperfectly imprinted on the mind by words, the sight of the animals doth it a thousand times better: and the idea of the particular colour of *gold*, is not to be got by any description of it, but only by the frequent exercise of the eyes about it, as is evident; in those who are used to this metal, who will frequently distinguish true from counterfeit, pure from adulterate, by the sight, where others (who have as good eyes, but yet, by use, have not got the precise nice idea of that peculiar yellow) shall not perceive any difference. The like may be said of those other simple ideas, peculiar in their kind to any substance; for which precise ideas, there are no peculiar names. The particular ringing sound there is in *gold*, distinct from the sound of other bodies, has no particular name annexed to it, no more than the particular yellow, that belongs to that metal.

The ideas of their powers best by definition §22. But because many of the simple ideas that make up our specific ideas of substances, are powers, which lie not obvious to our senses in the things as they ordinarily appear; therefore, *in the signification of our names of substances, some part of the signification will be better made known, by enumerating those simple ideas, than in showing the substance itself.* For he that, to the yellow shining colour of *gold* got by sight, shall, from my enumerating them, have the ideas of great ductility, fusibility, fixedness, and solubility, in *aqua regia*, will have a perfecter idea of *gold*, than he can have by seeing a piece of *gold*, and thereby imprinting in his mind only its obvious qualities. But if the formal constitution of this shining, heavy, ductile thing (from whence all these its properties flow) lay open to our senses, as the formal constitution, or essence of a triangle does, the signification of the word *gold*, might as easily be ascertained, as that of *triangle*.

§23. Hence we may take notice, how much the foundation of all *our knowledge of corporeal things, lies in our senses.* For how spirits, separate from bodies, (whose knowledge and ideas of these things, is certainly much more perfect than ours) know them, we have no notion, no idea at all. The whole extent of our knowledge, or imagination, reaches not beyond our own ideas, limited to our ways of perception. Though yet it be not to be doubted, that spirits of a higher rank than those immersed in flesh, may have as clear ideas of the radical constitution of substances, as we have of a triangle, and so perceive how all their properties and operations flow from thence: but the manner how they come by that knowledge, exceeds our conceptions.

A reflection on the knowledge of spirits

§24. But though definitions will serve to explain the names of substances, as they stand for our ideas; yet they leave

Ideas also of substances must be conformable to things

them not without great imperfection, as they stand for things. For our names of substances being not put barely for our ideas, but being made use of ultimately to represent things, and so are put in their place, their signification must agree with the truth of things, as well as with men's ideas. And therefore in substances, we are not always to rest in the ordinary complex idea, commonly received as the signification of that word, but must go a little further, and inquire into the nature and properties of the things themselves, and thereby perfect, as much as we can, our ideas of their distinct species; or else learn them from such as are used to that sort of things, and are experienced in them. For since 'tis intended their names should stand for such collections of simple ideas, as do really exist in things themselves, as well as for the complex idea in other men's minds, which in their ordinary acceptation they stand for: therefore *to define their names right, natural history is to be inquired into*; and their properties are, with care and examination, to be found out. For it is not enough, for the avoiding inconveniencies in discourses and arguings about natural bodies and substantial things, to have learned, from the propriety of the language, the common but confused, or very imperfect idea, to which each word is applied, and to keep them to that idea in our use of them: but we must, by acquainting ourselves with the history of that sort of things rectify and settle our complex idea, belonging to each specific name; and in discourse with others, (if we find them mistake us) we ought to tell, what the complex idea is, that we make such a name stand for. This is the more necessary to be done by all those, who search after knowledge, and philosophical verity, in that children being taught words whilst they have but imperfect notions of things, apply them at random, and without much thinking, and seldom frame determined ideas to be signified by them. Which custom, (it being easy, and serving well enough for the ordinary affairs of life and conversation) they are apt to continue, when they are men: and so begin at the wrong end, learning words first, and perfectly, but make the notions to which they apply those words afterwards, very overtly. By this means it comes to pass, that men speaking the proper language of their country, *i.e.* according to grammar-rules of that language, do yet speak very improperly of things themselves; and by their arguing one with another, make but small progress in the discoveries of useful truths, and the knowledge of things, as they are to be found in themselves, and not in our imaginations; and it matters not much, for the improvement of our knowledge, how they are called.

§25. It were therefore to be wished, that *Not easy to be* men, versed in physical inquiries, and *made so* acquainted with the several sorts of natural bodies, would set down those simple ideas, wherein they observe the individuals of each sort constantly to agree. This would remedy a great deal of that confusion, which comes from several persons, applying the same name to a collection of a smaller, or greater number of sensible qualities, proportionably as they have been more or less acquainted with, or accurate in examining the qualities of any sorts of things, which come under one denomination. But a dictionary of this sort, containing, as it were, a natural history, requires too many hands, as well as too much time, cost, pains, and sagacity, ever to be hoped for; and till that be done, we must content ourselves with such definitions of the names of substances, as explain the sense men use them in. And 'twould be well, where there is occasion, if they would afford us so much. This yet is not usually done; but men talk to one another, and dispute in words, whose meaning is not agreed between them, out of a mistake, that the signification of common words, are certainly established, and the precise ideas, they stand for, perfectly known; and that it is a shame to be ignorant of them. Both which suppositions are false: no names of complex ideas having so settled determined significations, that they are constantly used for the same precise ideas. Nor is it a shame for a man not to have a certain knowledge of anything, but by the necessary ways of attaining it; and so it is no discredit not to know, what precise idea any sound stands for in another man's mind, without he declare it to me, by some other way than barely using that sound, there being no other way, without such a declaration, certainly to know it. Indeed, the necessity of communication by language, brings men to an agreement in the signification of common words, within some tolerable latitude, that may serve for ordinary conversation: and so a man cannot be supposed wholly ignorant of the ideas, which are annexed to words by common use, in a language familiar to him. But common use, being but a very uncertain rule, which reduces itself at last to the ideas of particular men, proves often but a very variable standard. But though such a dictionary, as I have above-mentioned, will require too much time, cost and pains, to be hoped for in this age; yet, methinks, it is not unreasonable to propose, that words standing for things, which are known and distinguished by their outward shapes, should be expressed by little draughts and prints made of them. A vocabulary made after this fashion, would, perhaps with more ease, and in less time, teach the true signification of many terms, especially in languages of remote countries or ages, and settle truer ideas in men's minds of several things, whereof we read the names in ancient authors, than all the large and laborious comments of learned critics. Naturalists, that treat of plants and animals, have found the benefit of this way: and he that has had occasion to consult them, will have reason to confess, that he has a clear idea of *apium*, or *ibex* from a little print of that herb, or beast, than he could have from a long definition of the names of either of them. And so, no doubt, he would have of *strigil* and *sistrum*, if instead of a *curry-comb*, and *cymbal*, which are the English names dictionaries render them by, he could see stamped in the margin, small pictures of these instruments, as they were in use amongst the ancients. *Toga, tunica, pallium*, are words easily translated by *gown, coat*, and *cloak*: but we have thereby no more true ideas of the fashion of those habits amongst the Romans, than we have of the faces of the tailors who made them. Such things as these, which the eye distinguishes by their shapes, would be best let into the mind by draughts made of them, and more determine the signification of such words, than any other words set for them, or made use of to define them. But this only by the by.

§26. *Fifthly,* if men will not be at the pains to declare the meaning of their words, and definitions of their terms are not to be had; yet this is the least can be expected, that in all discourses, wherein one man pretends to instruct or convince another, he should *use the same word constantly in the same sense*: if this were done, (which nobody can refuse, without great disingenuity) many of the books extant might be spared; many of the controversies in dispute would be at an end; several of those great volumes, swollen with ambiguous words, now used in one sense, and by and by in another, would shrink into a very narrow compass; and many of the philosophers' (to mention no other,) as well as poets' works, might be contained in a nutshell.

§27. But after all, the provision of words is so scanty in respect of that infinite variety of thoughts, that men, wanting terms to suit their precise notion, will, notwithstanding their utmost caution, be forced often to use the same word, in somewhat different senses. And though in the continuation of a discourse, or the pursuit of an argument, there be hardly room to digress into a particular definition, as often as a man varies the signification of any term; yet the import of the discourse will, for the most part, if there be no designed fallacy, sufficiently lead candid and intelligent readers, into the true meaning of it: but where that is not sufficient to guide the reader, there it concerns the writer to explain his meaning, and show in what sense he there uses that term.

THE STORY OF PENGUIN CLASSICS

Before 1946 ...'Classics' are mainly the domain of academics and students, without readable editions for everyone else. This all changes when a little-known classicist, E. V. Rieu, presents Penguin founder Allen Lane with the translation of Homer's Odyssey that he has been working on and reading to his wife Nelly in his spare time.

1946 The Odyssey becomes the first Penguin Classic published, and promptly sells three million copies. Suddenly, classic books are no longer for the privileged few.

1950s Rieu, now series editor, turns to professional writers for the best modern, readable translations, including Dorothy L. Sayers's *Inferno* and Robert Graves's *The Twelve Caesars*, which revives the salacious original.

1960s 1961 sees the arrival of the Penguin Modern Classics, showcasing the best twentieth-century writers from around the world. Rieu retires in 1964, hailing the Penguin Classics list as 'the greatest educative force of the 20th century'.

1970s A new generation of translators arrives to swell the Penguin Classics ranks, and the list grows to encompass more philosophy, religion, science, history and politics.

1980s The Penguin American Library joins the Classics stable, with titles such as *The Last of the Mohicans* safeguarded. Penguin Classics now offers the most comprehensive library of world literature available.

1990s Penguin Popular Classics are launched, offering readers budget editions of the greatest works of literature. Penguin Audiobooks brings the classics to a listening audience for the first time, and in 1999 the launch of the Penguin Classics website takes them online to an ever larger global readership.

The 21st Century Penguin Classics are rejacketed for the first time in nearly twenty years. This world famous series now consists of more than 1,300 titles, making the widest range of the best books ever written available to millions – and constantly redefining the meaning of what makes a 'classic'.

The Odyssey continues ...

The best books ever written

PENGUIN ⊕ CLASSICS

SINCE 1946